Beyond the

Of course, anyone would want to wake up from a really bad dream - especially one that seemed like it may never end, while successively stripping away joys and conveniences of our modern living.

The COVID-19 pandemic bestowed on us a collective nightmare experience of varying intensity, akin to a "Black Swan" event, as author and mathematical philosopher Nassim Taleb might describe—given its universal rarity and devastating effects and seeming predictability in hindsight. However, we may remember this remarkable time in our history rather as a "White Swan" event—one that catalyzed a more common occurrence of evolving Environmental, Social, and Governance (ESG) principles, a mainstreaming of sustainability—fueled by the digital innovations that designed ways to survive and thrive into a new, and more holistic, world order.

Now, as we emerge from the remnants of the pandemic's aftermath, we find ourselves at the late dawn of a new geologic epoch—the "Anthropocene"—where the impact of humans on the planet's geology and ecosystems looms so monumentally that the gravest threat to our existence stems from our own actions. Contained within these pages, you will discover insights from leaders across diverse domains—community, industry, public administration, and the investment community. Through their own experiences, we unfurl "White Swan sightings"— moments when sustainability flourished in response to reverberations of the COVID-19 virus.

More poignantly, the journey ahead carries us beyond the realm of the Black Swan, while the acceleration of digital innovations equips us to herald a new era out of the Anthropocene and into a new one, with sustainability innovations as a critical placemat. The humanistic seismic shifts caused by the Pandemic will generate a future of holistic interoperability between digital and organic matters. We are on the brink of designing unprecedented harmony with each other and equilibrium of regenerative growth with the world around us. The urgency has never been greater, nor the possibilities so profound.

Beyond the Black Swan

How the Pandemic and Digital Innovations Intensified the Sustainability Imperative – Everywhere

Rika Nakazawa

Routledge
Taylor & Francis Group
A PRODUCTIVITY PRESS BOOK

First published 2024
by Routledge
605 Third Avenue, New York, NY 10158

and by Routledge
4 Park Square, Milton Park, Abingdon, Oxon, OX14 4RN

Routledge is an imprint of the Taylor & Francis Group, an Informa business

© 2024 Rika Nakazawa

ISBN: 9781032611693 (hbk)
ISBN: 9781032611686 (pbk)
ISBN: 9781003462347 (ebk)

DOI: 10.4324/9781003462347

Typeset in Minion
by Deanta Global Publishing Services, Chennai, India

Contents

Preface

WAKING UP

A nightmare—what the pandemic seems to us now. We can almost remember that day that somehow seems both like a million years ago, as well as just yesterday: those early days when civilization warped—with cities shutting down, borders closing, gloves and masks becoming required fashion, and the hoarding of toilet paper commenced.

Thanks to a deadly virus particle not that much smaller than a wildfire smoke particle (see Figure 0.1), the entire world became a giant experiment for how we were going to confront, adapt to, and build resilience to a threat to our very existence. Figure 0.1[1] shows just how tiny this catalyst of mass disruption is in comparison to other miniscule particles.

This specter that we all shared—though with varying degrees of impact—enacted dramatic change across every facet of our lives. In that way, some might consider COVID-19 to be a "Black Swan" event, à la Nassim Taleb. Taleb coined the term Black Swan in his seminal work, *The Black Swan: The Impact of the Highly Improbable*, published in 2007, positing that Black Swan events were rare and often devastating outlier events that were perhaps predictable in hindsight. The moniker represented the historical context where black swans were and are rarely seen. The dramatic impact of the pandemic manifested in millions of deaths, debilitating illness, social isolation, mental illness, supply chain chaos ... the list continues endlessly. History books are still to be written on all the devastation that the pandemic has wrought, along with a series of social and political aftermath effects that may thread through generations to come.

Yet, yet ... amidst the darkness there are bright points of light. The roots of this trace back unusually to my ongoing work in advancing gender and racial diversity in business at large, and more specifically in the technology industry. In 2019, after a stark epiphany at Princeton's Women Alumni Conference, I embarked on an entrepreneurial side hustle.

FIGURE 0.1

Comparison of the COVID-19 particle relative to other micro particles

During a session at the conference that illuminated the dearth of women on corporate boards, I resolved to do whatever I could to use the power of technology to help women build "social capital" (a fancy way to reference a "professional but social" network), which I saw as a critical catalyst for women to gain access to the corporate boardroom.

That resolve resulted in the creation of this side hustle that took the shape of a digital platform, called BoardSeatMeet (now known as STRIDES AI). As part of the requisite lean and agile approach to building STRIDES, I talked to many board leaders and embarked on a comprehensive board training program at UCLA's Anderson School of Business specifically targeted at women corporate board leaders.

The inspiration I gleaned from these conversations and interviews triggered my foray into book writing, with my first book *Dear Chairwoman*, published in March 2021, which became an Amazon bestseller on the day of publication. Through the book, I dove into the experiences of women business leaders and chronicled their journey to the boardroom as a way to advance and celebrate diversity in an era of gender equity transformation—without realizing the exposure it would give me to an era of even greater change.

For almost a full year preceding the pandemic, I basically had a front row seat to learning about the critical success factors for enterprise growth and success through the lens of corporate board directors. And as my engagement in this pinnacle of corporate governance continued with the onset of COVID-19, I started to see the acronym "ESG" emerge with greater frequency and intensity. I noticed that issues around climate change (the E for Environment), social equity (the S for Social), and the Governance needed for global communities and businesses alike seemed to grow in intensity and focus.

In parallel, as I started traveling again in 2021 as permitted (initially to visit my ailing father in Tokyo), I saw advertisements and public notices that addressed sustainability increasing in prominence and frequency. Ads like the one in Figure 0.2 by airlines appeared not just on the planes, but in airports and runways.[2]

Also advertisements from global banks (Figure 0.3).[3]

And from leading technology companies (Figure 0.4).[4]

That was when I thought that maybe, just maybe, the Black Swan of COVID-19 had triggered "White Swan" moments—a time when positive discourse around social equity and climate change would no longer be

FIGURE 0.2
United Airlines advertisement touting sustainability in United Airlines operations

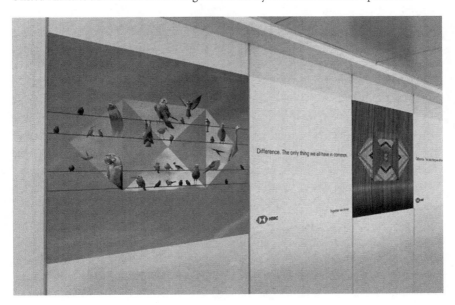

FIGURE 0.3
Advertisement from HSBC with DEI messaging

FIGURE 0.4
DELL promoting commitment to sustainability

"outlier" topics embedded in CSR reports or confined to corners of the United Nations Sustainable Development Goals (SDGs), Conference of the Parties (commonly known as COP), and the placemat to NGOs and non-profits. Perhaps the pandemic that was so devastating in many ways also catalyzed sustainability in the form of ESG vernacular to shift out of the corners and edges of "do good" and "socially responsible" themes, but to a mainstream field of view. In other words, could we see the pandemic as not just a "Black Swan" event, but also something that created "White Swan" series of mainstream sustainability moments. Could we remember the pandemic for having positive amplification effects for sustainable business, communities, and nation states.

To test my hypothesis, I embarked on a series of interviews in 2022 with leaders across multinational enterprises, local communities, academia, venture capital, startup, and government. The intent of the interviews was to capture anecdotes and stories in response to the opening question:

> *I think the pandemic led to the intensification of the focus on sustainability in community, business, and national governments, and largely accelerated by technology and the digitalization of how we work, live, and play.*
> *Do you agree, and if you do, why do you think that is, and what have you experienced—personally and/or professionally—around that idea?*

With the interviews, I sought to get beneath the headlines that are so often captivated by big brands and cults of personalities. Most of all, this was an opportunity to not let the social experiment of the pandemic go to waste. It allowed us to leverage the impact of one existential crisis with one that is, in my humble and now more knowledgeable position, even greater, and to demonstrate the ability of all of us to commit to thriving together as a global community on this Earth.

Through the course of writing this book, I was also exploring a master's degree at the convergence of sustainability, business, and technology. That exploration did not yield much. There was not a single textbook that thoroughly brought forward these conjoined agendas of the pandemic, digital innovation, and sustainability. I saw the need for a book that will reshape both the way we might remember the pandemic and highlight how it catalyzed the paradigm shift that may just be what saves us from ourselves. I do not mean to say that this is that book—but I do want it to be part of the conversation.

Through the research on this book, I looked for "White Swan sightings"— empirical examples that belie how COVID-19 ignited a dramatic acceleration toward climate impact, social equity, and global governance. As I went through the interviews, I found clustered (and as you will see overlapping) patterns across five key themes of "impact to and influence of": Technology, Community, Governance and Government, Corporate and Industry, and Investment.

We first explore **technology**'s role in this acceleration of the sustainability agenda, especially in the context of the other four themes. Digitalization plays a role in accountability for corporate sustainability goals and opens possibilities for entities committing to sustainability to be held more accountable. Emerging technologies can drive the capturing, reporting, and quantifying of the impact of sustainability impact and outcomes.

Then we dive into the increased power of **community-driven movements**, looking to see what lessons we might take from them. In particular, we focus on Black Lives Matter, the ways that Diversity, Equity and Inclusion (DEI) revitalized, and the rise of blockchain applications as key examples of community-driven movements driving business and societal change during, and after, the COVID pandemic.

Third, we examine how **governance and governments** were impacted and influenced the rise of sustainability initiatives. We see how these initiatives were catalyzed by the need for better private and public partnerships in the face of massive disruption, and the opportunity to transform organizations and societies with an agenda that equips them to be more resilient and sustainable.

Fourth, we traverse the expanse of the **investment** ecosystem in responding to, and being influenced by, the conflation of risk and sustainability that was heightened by the pandemic. In this segment, we also uncover a new consideration of wealth as the sectors like "climate tech" and "green energy" blossom with the tailwinds of post-pandemic recovery.

And finally, we explore **corporate impact and influence**, and the industrialization of sustainability. Every enterprise in every industry experienced a near complete annihilation of "business as usual." Operational risk had to be refactored, the management of people recalibrated, and more profoundly, the purpose of their existence revisited.

Through this journey of *Beyond the Black Swan*, I anticipate that you will observe the way communities, businesses, and governments are on a remarkable path of agency for a sustainable future, since the onset of the pandemic. As devastating as the coronavirus has been for so many, and the strong desire for us to move past the lingering nightmarish memories of how the 2020 decade kicked off, I hope the "White Swan sightings" (moments where sustainability actions were taken at any scale—from individual to global organizations) throughout these pages turn on some high beams onto our collective existence and illuminate previously dimmed corners of our humanity. *Beyond the Black Swan* is intended to be energizing and empowering and to spark the kind of multilogue we need in a post-pandemic era of a new way for us to thrive—with all organisms great and small. This energy and empowerment, together with breakthrough digital innovation accelerated by the pandemic, will be critical for how we transition swiftly to a collective experience that is defined by elevated intelligence and sustainable interoperability with the world around us.

NOTES

1. Credit: Visual Capitalist. https://www.visualcapitalist.com/visualizing-relative-size-of-particles/
2. https://onemileatatime.com/news/united-good-leads-the-way-ad/
3. TBD
4. @Rika Nakazawa

Acknowledgements

Don't sit this one out. Do something. You are by accident of fate alive at an absolutely critical moment in the history of our planet.

– Carl Sagan

In the vast tapestry of human experience, we stand upon the shoulders of countless visionaries and seekers of truth. To each of these brilliant minds I encountered in the research for the book, whose intellectual constellations have illuminated the path we tread, I extend my deepest appreciation.

Alison Taylor	Denise Gershbein	Lawrence Chu	Ron Epperson
Alvin Wang	Diana Rakus	Luis Neves	Sagie Davidovich
Andreas Sjostrom	Gavriella Schuster	Maneesh Sharma	Shivam Kishore
Baiju Shah	George Coehlo	Mani Balakrishnan	Sonia Consiglio Favaretto
Barbara Adachi	Gill Pratt	Mary de Wysocki	Steve Ramseur
Ben Way	Ivo Timoteo	Mark Deuitch	Stephen Clarke
Bill Weihl	Jaslyn Wang	Mike Burns	Steve Young
Bracken Darrell	Jason Salfi	Mona ElNagger	Sue Lawton
Brent Waechter	Jason Vazanno	Naoko Okumoto	Tonie Hansen
Carla Bailo	Jen Cohen	Naomi Koshi	Tracy Barba
Carolina Aguilar	Jenifer Rogers	Noha White	Vito Mabrucco
Caroline Chan	Jim Adler	Philippe Cases	Xavier Denoly
Ceah Justice	Josh Goldenberg	Praveen Shankar	Xavone Charles
Christine Tiballi	Kaoru Inoue	Rachel Payne	Youngcho Chi
Cooper Heffner	Kate Gallego	Rahul Sekhon	Yuriko Koike
David Ellington	Kevin Grayling	Rene Haas	Yvonne Wolf
David Eun	Kim Yapchai	Roli Agrawal	

A special note of gratitude to the "White Swan Mastermind Group" who came together at the beginning of this project when it was just a Eureka moment. Thank you for your confidence, spirit, energy, and generous contribution of time and effort: Ako Shimada, Amy Peck, Andrijana Cvetkovik, Claudine Goldsmith, Jackie Steele, Joanne Fedeyko, Larry Doyle, Marjan Khanji, Marko Simic, Martha Cotton, Pavlina Yankieva, and Tarik Heitmann. And an earnest thank you to my change-making

NTT colleagues who are tireless stewards of a thriving future for industry, communities and all living beings. Akiko Kudo, Abhijit Dubey, Yoshiko Ikeda, David Costa, Kazu Gomi, Brandon Lee, Warren Small, Vicky Bullivant, Albi van Zyl, Vab Goel, Robb Rasmussen, Bob Pryor, Marv Mouchawar, Kayo Ito, Miriam Murphy, John Lombard, Theresa Jones, Vijay Sahrawat, Shahid Ahmed, Tanvir Khan, Akhil Uniyal, Zellah Fuphe, Sai Sekar, Stephen Kelly, Eric Clark, Megan Dahlgren, Maria Metz, Zaif Siddiqi, Sai Sekar, Sumukh Tendulkar, Noa Asher, Corie Pierce, Jacques Bonifay, Bertrand Salomon, Terri Hatcher, Christine Barr, Mona Charif, Dee Smith, Kai Grunwitz, Parm Sandhu, Gioconda Di Gennaro, Fabio Santos, Stephen Green, Chris Shaw, Kyoko Sugiyama, Ryoko Shintaku, Shu Ikeda, Michelle Killebrew, Roberto del Corno, Florence Hugon, Leticia Lastra, Brian Wilson, Wolf Stinnes, Bill Baver, Bennett Indart, Nathan Hart, Devin Yaung, Mino Umehara, María Jesús Villa García, Siri Nakprasit, Allison Bass, Martin Schauder, Stuart Crawford-Browne, Joanna Miro are among many, many others at NTT embody or advance the convergence of sustainable innovation and breakthrough possibilities.

Furthermore, I would like to acknowledge the invaluable production contributions from Yuiko Sugino (book cover design), Jenn LeBlanc, and Linda Popky.

Finally, thank you from all of my ♥ to Dawson—for being my fearless collaborator and ardent partner in this journey of discovery, change, impact, and boundless possibilities. Per Carl Sagan, we are most definitely not sitting this one out. Indeed, I dare say we are fiercely undertaking not just "something," but "all-the-things," together.

About the Author

Rika Nakazawa is a senior technology executive, VC investor, best-selling author, and frequent public speaker on technology-powered industry transformation. She is Group Vice President within NTT's New Ventures & Innovation team where she is focusing on advancing key emerging technologies like 5G, Edge Computing, and IoT across global enterprises. In her additional role as Head of Sustainability for NTT Americas, Rika is driving NTT's sustainability ambition in operations while also orchestrating the go-to-market for NTT's climate-positive solutions across their portfolio of digital infrastructure solutions. For two consecutive years in 2022 and 2023, Rika has been awarded "Power 70" and "Power 80" recognition for the Women of Channel awards with The Channel Co's CRN network. She has also been ranked as "Top 100 in Emerging Tech" by Women of the Future.

Trilingual in Japanese, German, and English, Rika grew up in Japan and moved to the United States to attend Princeton University. Rika has since worked internationally in senior executive roles in strategy, business development, consulting, and marketing with Fortune 500 companies—Accenture, NVIDIA, Capgemini, Sony—and Silicon Valley startups. She is a Digital Innovation veteran and has served on multiple boards in Next-Gen Computing, XR/VR/AR, Cybersecurity, and AI ecosystems. By summer 2024, Rika will have attained her Master's degree in Sustainable Business Leadership (a combined Master of Science in Environment and Master in Business Administration degree) from the University of Leeds in the UK.

Rika is a co-founder of STRIDES AI, a social impact venture leveraging AI to establish genuine connections between under-represented talent and enterprises to achieve socioeconomic equity, and a non-executive Director on the board of Venus Shell Systems—a blue economy enterprise. She is also the best-selling author of *Dear Chairwoman*, featuring the trials and triumphs of women corporate board leaders. The book achieved Amazon's bestseller status on the day of launch and has been translated and published by Diamond Publishing in Japan.

1

Technology: Digital Saturation

BYTE-SIZED BITS

The pandemic heralded an era of what we might call "the Great Digitalization." More assets (content/data) became *digitized*, while processes and systems become more *digitalized*—by a factor that will continue for some time to come. The impact of this double "d" development means that digital technology enablers (systems, hardware, data center, etc.) need to account for the expanded energy consumption on the one side to power an increasingly wider array of ecosystems, while also being an agent in ways that emerging technology can support achieving sustainability outcomes. This dichotomy presents a fundamental distinction—the notion of "Green IT" versus "IT for Green"—that shapes the landscape of technological advancement in relation to sustainability impacts.

Our e-savior

As we've all experienced firsthand, the widespread adoption of digital access and connectivity played a crucial role in adapting to a new way of life and work. The COVID-19 pandemic's stay-at-home and lockdown measures made digital technology an integral part of both our professional and everyday routines. A report jointly published by Hootsuite and We Are Social in July 2020 shed light on the significant impact of digital platforms and devices during this period.

DOI: 10.4324/9781003462347-1

According to the survey,[1] there was an impressive 8+% increase in internet users and a solid 10% surge in active social media users worldwide. Various connected devices, including smartphones, laptops, tablets, and game consoles, experienced a remarkable rise in usage. Notably, 70% of internet users between the ages of 16 and 64 relied more heavily on their mobile phones, while nearly 50% reported increased usage of laptops due to the COVID-19 pandemic.

Delving into the reasons behind this trend, we discover the invaluable role of digital connectivity and access in helping people cope across a wide range of activities, including work, leisure, homecare, and more. The same survey conducted by Hootsuite and We Are Social revealed that a staggering 83% of respondents credited internet-connected devices for assisting them in dealing with the challenges posed by COVID-19-related lockdowns.

Meanwhile, over 50% of respondents confirmed that digital technology helped them cope in various ways, such as:

- Facilitating their children's education.
- Keeping them connected with friends and family.
- Supporting their job responsibilities (especially for white-collar workers).
- Providing entertainment and engagement for their children.

Without a doubt, digital tools played a pivotal role in enabling individuals to adapt and navigate through the pandemic's difficulties in both their personal and professional lives.

While "remote work" and "back-to-office" were the words that dominated headlines around the impact and aftermath of the pandemic, in the early days of COVID-19 "helps me do my job" was outpaced by "helps with my children's education," and easily trumped by "helps me cope" with COVID-related lockdowns—these were clear indicators of the disruptions caused by the pandemic to how we all work, live, and play.

The digitalization of connectivity, both socially and professionally, is evident in striking statistics, such as the meteoric rise of Zoom. Just a startup a mere decade ago, Zoom has now become a household and office-space name. Prior to the pandemic (around December 2019), it had approximately 10 million users. However, within a year, that number skyrocketed to an astounding 350 million users.[2] Notably, its revenue for 2020 surged by an impressive 400% compared to the previous year.

The Hootsuite survey also highlighted the increased use of digital devices, further reinforcing the trend. It comes as no surprise that Apple achieved a historic milestone during the pandemic. In August 2020, it became the first company to reach a staggering two trillion US dollar valuation.[3] This surge in valuation can be attributed to the widespread demand for new devices or upgrades to cope with the challenges of the pandemic, seeking solace, enhancing productivity, and staying connected.

From Trains, Planes, and Automobiles—To Teams and Zoom

Throughout our book, numerous leaders emphasized the profound impact of the pandemic on our embrace of digitalization, leading to increased transparency and the ability to demonstrate outcomes and impacts that inspire action, imitation, and the evolution of solutions.

Sonia Consiglio Favaretto, from the United Nations Global Compact, highlighted how heightened digital interconnectivity has transformed the way global teams collaborate. "Digitalization has compelled everyone to adapt to remote work, learning how to navigate this new landscape and become better human beings," she reflected. Favaretto further emphasized that the pandemic has made the world feel smaller, highlighting our shared humanity. "From health crises to social issues, environmental concerns, and economies in lockdown … this interconnectedness has brought Environmental, Social, and Governance (ESG) topics to the forefront of discussions, as we have concretely realized the interdependence of our world."

Lawrence Chu, Managing Director at Moelis & Company, emphasized something we all experienced, but perhaps had not fully internalized. With technology, we could work remotely (thank you, Microsoft Teams, Zoom, Google Meet), and not contribute to carbon emissions from fossil fuel consumption from driving, flying, and taking other modes of transportation. In fact, the opportunity to work remotely, and to have a blended life of home and work, may be amplifying our very productivity. "It also allows us to harness the intelligence—the power that is America or globally—and it allows people to be productive in a manner that wasn't there necessarily before," he noted. Could it be that the pandemic both enabled us to be more sustainable in how we worked AND yet more productive?

At the same time, Chu pointed to how this increased digitalization has made us more aware of where there are gaps, where those gaps limit opportunities, and how these need to be part of the accountability conversation. He specifically pointed to how the pandemic exposed the digital divide, noting the challenges around gender and social equity from a historically contextualized lack of access to "social capital." We address the impact of greater access to social capital enabled by digital technologies in our chapter on the theme of corporate impact and influence in Chapter 3.

It's a Small (Digital) World After All

With one fell swoop of a pandemic, digital DNA has become more than ever firmly embedded into how we operate. David Eun, former Chief Innovation Office for Samsung, remarked in our conversation,

> At one point, every company said, "This digital thing will be something," so we'll have the IT people handle digital. Then maybe we'll have a Chief Digital Officer, and we'll send him or her over in some corner and allow them to have some small team or they'll manage our website. I think what people realize now is digital is just part of the fabric of your whole business. You have CEOs who have just grown up through the system and understand how it all sort of knits together.

In the enterprise world, we find ourselves on the cusp of the next phase of digital transformation, building upon the evolutionary journey from Web 1.0 to mobile, cloud computing, and beyond. This current phase represents a tangible manifestation of what we refer to as the "metaverse." Coined by Neal Stephenson in his 1992 book *Snow Crash*, the term now encapsulates the concept of interconnected 3D virtual worlds that facilitate social and economic interactions. The integration of these elements will shape a new era characterized by connected devices, connected individuals, and the intricate interplay of data, connectivity, and intelligence. In June 2023, Stephenson took the stage at the Augmented World Expo in Silicon Valley, where he alluded to the recent advancements that have paved the way for the development of a metaverse, without directly attributing these advancements to the pandemic's impact on digitization and digitalization. He remarked, "In just the past couple of years, it feels like numerous pieces of the puzzle have fallen into place—the prerequisites necessary for us to truly embark on the construction of a metaverse."[4]

HTC, a pioneering force in shaping the evolution of the metaverse, is at the forefront of driving its adoption in both the consumer and enterprise sectors. In our conversation with Alvin Wang, China President and Global VP of Corporate Development at HTC, he emphasized the transformative potential of merging virtual experiences with the physical world to enhance various aspects of our lives, be it work, education, or home life. Wang highlighted a study conducted by HTC in collaboration with universities during the early stages of the pandemic, which revealed significant findings regarding the impact of blending the digital and physical realms, also known as "spatial computing":

- Spatial collaboration enhances productivity and streamlines processes.
- Virtual workspaces foster greater satisfaction and a sense of belonging among teams.
- Students exhibit improved learning outcomes, better retention, and perform better in assessments when exposed to complex topics through virtual experiences.

Addressing the domain of education, Wang believes that the development of the metaverse holds immense potential for promoting educational equity. It enables students to access enriched experiences and information, both visually and spatially, that were previously only available to those with the financial means in the physical world. Wang envisions this elevation of educational standards and diversification of experiences leading to positive outcomes in politics, business, and industry.

With this "metaverse-ification" of our lives, we can leverage the hypergrowth of virtualization to tackle other key sustainability challenges as, for example, defined by the United Nations (UN) Sustainable Development Goals (SDGs). Established by the UN in 2015, the UN SDGs (see Figure 1.1) are a collection of 17 interlinked objectives designed to serve, as the UN describes, as a "shared blueprint for peace and prosperity for people and the planet, now and into the future."[5]

The UN SDGs serve as a comprehensive framework for promoting sustainable development in our interconnected global community, as demonstrated by the rapid spread of the pandemic. These goals encompass economic, ecological, and social dimensions, and each one represents a significant area of focus. The aim is that by leveraging the increasing

FIGURE 1.1
The United Nations Sustainable Development Goals

integration of digital technology and processes within industries, governments, and communities, we can more effectively address these complex challenges. The widespread adoption of digital tools and platforms provides us with an opportunity to tackle the SDGs with greater agility and scalability.

Fortunately, we had the chance to cross paths with Shivam Kishore, Senior Advisor, Digital Transformation with the UN Environment Program. Kishore's background maps well to the intersection of the UN SDGs to digital innovation. With a degree that combines engineering, environmental management, and law, and an initial career path in management consulting with large technology and financial organizations before joining the UN, Kishore reflected on where we are today as we emerge into a different landscape around the role of digital for sustainable business, government, and global collaboration. He shared,

> A lot of governmental organizations, corporate organizations, and academia, are viewing sustainability and tech as two different independent streams. There's a lot of conversations and ability to do a lot of composition on tech. The consideration is that tech is a very integral part of the world we live in today. In fact, we live in a digital economy, so sustainability and techniques can be dissected better. Where how does sustainability impact? Second, how to take you back to the ability. So, for us, very important work is how do we build capacities where countries, corporations, and individuals can start to realize outcomes through sustainability centered tech.

During our discussion on the role of technology and innovation in achieving sustainability goals, Kishore offered a balanced perspective, emphasizing the importance of understanding the context in which technology is applied. He highlighted,

> When we talk about things getting worse or better, we need to consider the specific issue at hand. In terms of social and environmental equity, technology in its current state has the potential to enable improvements in these areas. We are witnessing this transformation firsthand.

Kishore acknowledged the benefits of technology but also stressed the need for caution regarding its potential side effects. He drew an analogy, stating, "Technology is like a tool, just like a knife. We have learned as a society to use knives effectively in the kitchen, but for those who don't handle them properly, harm can occur." In this context, it is not the technology itself that is the determining factor, but rather its intentional application to address environmental, ecological, and social challenges. Given the interconnectedness of the global economy, the ability to achieve resilience and prosperity for all depends on leveraging technology for intentional positive outcomes.

Minding the (Digital Divide) Gap

The "Great Digitalization" was not evenly distributed, even while the impact of the pandemic seemed to be spreading and causing sickness and death indiscriminate of economic levels of race, culture, community, region, or country. Talking about connectivity and how we now live in a digital world, Praveen Shankar, managing partner at Ernst & Young, spoke about how the pandemic emphasized the digital divide—those who had access to information and those who did not.

"The problem was huge in the UK," Shankar said. "20% of the people did not have the devices to access online teaching, and then it's not everywhere that you have a proper internet connection. So that digital inclusion part also is so important."

Shankar agreed on the role that the pandemic played in making the topic mainstream: "It's like there's a new electricity, and when we talk about it in the UK, people talk about leveling up, and everything is being given priority." Digital connectivity and access to information and data became quite precious. "In fact," Shankar said, "we did a survey last year with small and medium enterprises, and we said, 'Hey, do you want digital infrastructure or physical infrastructure? Which one do you prefer?' Only 17% preferred physical over digital infrastructure."

Digitization democratizes the ability to input information into systems, and conversely extract data from systems and run improved analytical models—this was abundantly clear during the pandemic. More digitization of data and the digitalization of processes are also enabling a better understanding of causal loops toward sustainability outcomes. Causal loops are a way to demonstrate how various variables in a system are interrelated. One phrase that encapsulates the data-dependent nature of causal links comes from Alan Turing, who in 1950 remarked, "The displacement of a single electron by a billionth of a centimeter at one moment might make the difference between a man being killed by an avalanche a year later or escaping."[6] Now, the most recent and dramatic example of causal links and loops is the pandemic itself. One tiny protein particle unleashed a sequence of events and interdependencies so stark that governments had to lock people indoors and close borders. In many ways, the risk propensity of one act to the impact of a total whole can also be applied to sustainability, and the precedent set by the pandemic made this fragility of the Earth systems ever clearer.

Is There a Catch?

Thanks to the Great Digitalization, the pandemic saw a burst of emerging technologies. Gartner's "2021–2023 Emerging Technology Roadmap for Large Enterprises"[7] depicts dozens of technologies each across six vectors: Network, Security, Digital Workplace, IT Automation, Storage and Database, Computer Infrastructure and Platform Services. The roadmap delineates how each of these technologies are on a lifecycle from "In Planning" to "Deployment Completion" by 2021—right toward the end of the pandemic. From Software-Defined Storage to Edge Networking to IoT Platform and more, we have the hope shared in several interviews that this burst of digital innovation will help us achieve complex but critical ESG ambitions. Meanwhile, the environmental effects of Information Technology (IT) or Information and Communication Technologies (ICT) are subject to debate. On the one hand, ICT is considered a contributor to rising levels of CO_2 emissions due to the production of machinery and devices—from energy consumption, and electronic waste recycling. For example, according to the International Energy Agency, data transmission networks consumed between 1.1 and 1.4% of global electricity at the height of the pandemic, in 2021.[8] Yet, these same technologies also hold the potential to mitigate CO_2 emissions on a global scale through the deployment of the technologies toward intelligent cities, transportation systems, electrical grids, industrial processes, and more.

Mary de Wysocki, the Chief Sustainability Officer at Cisco, demonstrated the ways that technology pioneers, like Cisco, are tacking these two opposite effects. For context, Cisco has been publishing Corporate Social Responsibility (CSR) reports since 2005, which include Cisco's commitment to environmental sustainability, and engaged cross-functional teams to set out goals and report on progress. Around the time the pandemic began, de Wysocki shared that given growing interest from our employees and increasing requests to share our net zero GHG goals and other sustainability commitments, Cisco identified our purpose to "Power an Inclusive Future for All." And as we started going down that path, the Chief Sustainability officer role was formalized to manage the ways we would meet the expectations of our teams, our customers, our investors, our partners—the vast ecosystem in which we operate.

Part of de Wysocki's teams' remit is not to also advance a circular economy initiative with a "Take Back" program with their partners—where they offer discounts on new equipment while simultaneously taking back the used equipment for recycling and refurbishment. de Wysocki sees this program gathering steam and the merits of circular economy contribute to their customers' own sustainability ambitions.

Post-Pandemic World Clock: Tech-Tock, Tech-Tock

In the same way that digital content and devices helped us cope as communities while a miniscule particle wreaked havoc on our lives, we can anticipate that digital innovation will help us confront this bigger existential threat than the virus—the combination of instabilities caused by climate change, social inequity, and the socio-political crisis that started to feature more prominently during the pandemic. With the Internet of Things (IoT) interchangeably called the Internet of Everything (IoE), bright engineers and industrial designers are threading the ways industry can baseline, measure, analyze, and action on the full lifecycle of sustainability metrics—from greenhouse gas (GHG) emissions to water management, waste and pollution management, energy consumption, and of other ESG metrics as relevant to stakeholders of an organization.

During our conversation with Rene Haas, CEO of ARM Holdings, he acknowledged the profound integration of technology into the human experience, particularly emphasized by the pandemic. As a prominent chip and semiconductor design enterprise, ARM has played a crucial role in the evolution and increasing importance of semiconductors in our highly digitalized societies and businesses. Throughout the pandemic, the industry faced significant supply chain challenges, and ARM, as a key player in the silicon chip ecosystem, was not immune to these disruptions. Still, semiconductor chips have become ubiquitous, powering a wide range of devices from automobiles and smartphones to televisions, and forming the foundation for the interconnectedness of the digital world, paving the way toward the era of "Smart _____."

ARM has made tremendous progress in innovation around IP and semiconductors, particularly in terms of carbon footprint and sustainable innovation, and Haas's explanation of this is awe-inspiring. "Basically," Haas said,

> the IP we license is the CPU or brain that goes in any appliance. Where we've had our success historically, has been smartphones. So literally 100% of the smartphones on the planet use ARM as the CPU of the brain. All Android phones, all iOS phones—100% of those are all ARM-based.

Haas added,

> one of the reasons that make ARM really good for smartphones is the smartphone is a computer in your hands. It needs very high computational power, but it needs really low energy consumption. It needs to run off the battery, and it needs to run for a long time.

That translates to several other settings, as well, as Haas noted.

> When you think about next-generation devices like cloud data centers or autonomous automotive electric vehicles, those are great setups for ARM because a data center, candidly, needed as much computing power as you can possibly put into a fixed amount of square footage, [with a] fixed quantities of kilowatts and megawatts going into the plan. ARM, which was traditionally not known for being very successful in the data center, now has a huge footprint with Amazon Web Services (AWS).

ARM's technology also has a significant role to play in the automotive industry's pursuit of sustainability. Haas highlighted that ARM's presence can be found in approximately 30 chips within a typical vehicle. This traces back to the early days of ARM when it was known as Acorn, specifically designed to power devices like the original Palm Pilot and Apple's Newton, which served as Apple's first personal digital assistant (PDA) three decades ago. These origins established ARM's expertise in delivering high computing performance within a compact form factor.

Haas emphasized that ARM's extensive experience not only provides a clear playbook for automotive applications but also presents a compelling sustainability story. By enabling efficient and powerful computing capabilities in vehicles, ARM's technology contributes to the development of sustainable transportation solutions. The integration of ARM chips in automobiles not only supports performance and functionality but also aligns with the industry's growing emphasis on reducing environmental impact and achieving greater energy efficiency.

ARM chips find application in augmented glasses and even augmented reality contact lenses, according to Haas. He specifically mentioned Mojo Vision, a company that integrates ARM chips into its augmented reality contact lenses. These lenses, when worn, provide a heads-up display for firefighters and military personnel, allowing them to navigate through challenging environments like smoke-filled areas. Haas anticipates that such applications will become increasingly prevalent in the future. He envisions a generation of individuals, particularly children, who will be more comfortable with wearing these advanced devices and interacting with the world in this augmented manner. The use of ARM technology in augmented glasses and contact lenses represents an exciting frontier in merging technology and human perception, opening new possibilities for broader access to enhanced experiences.

Amidst the focus on cutting-edge technology, Haas and others emphasized the importance of striking a balance between technological advancements and preserving our human experience. They acknowledged that while technology brings many benefits, there are certain aspects of human interaction that cannot be substituted or replicated. Haas highlighted this perspective, stating, "On the flip side, there's no substitute. There are just some things that technology cannot replace and cannot be relative to human interaction." It serves as a reminder that, despite technological progress, nurturing and maintaining genuine human connections remain essential for a successful and meaningful life.

Sustainably, Just for You

Innovation and technology have historically played a vital role in helping societies overcome various calamities throughout human history. One such development, Lean Manufacturing, has resurfaced in the hyper-digitalized post-pandemic landscape, expanding its influence into driving sustainability through digital innovation and enhancing personalized experiences. This exciting phenomenon was brought to life in our discussion with Mani Balakrishnan, Chief Sustainability Officer at Zebra Technologies.

Lean manufacturing is a systematic approach to production that prioritizes maximizing value for end users while minimizing waste and inefficiencies. Originating in post-World War II Japan during the country's economic rebuilding phase, Toyota sought ways to optimize its manufacturing processes in the face of resource constraints, such as limited raw materials and a shortage of skilled labor. The focus was on eliminating waste, reducing costs, and improving productivity.

As a chemical engineer with a strong commitment to sustainability, Balakrishnan brings a unique perspective to the table. He envisions promoting resource efficiency, reducing waste, and mitigating the environmental impact of industrial processes. During our conversation, he emphasized how the digital transformation accelerated by the pandemic has further advanced sustainability in manufacturing, transitioning from mass production to personalized production.

The seamless and swift flow of data in today's digital systems enables products and services to be curated according to individual needs and preferences at a large scale. This personalization approach translates to less waste in the product lifecycle and delivers enhanced experiences and outcomes for end users. Balakrishnan highlighted the profound impact of digitalization, stating, "There's a much deeper impact than simply manufacturing EVs and other products to tackle efficiency and waste. It's fundamentally about addressing the demand economy ... People now seek more tailored, customized products that meet their specific expectations." Digitalization has made this level of personalization more possible than ever before.

Calamity is the Mother of Innovation

In some ways, the transformation we are witnessing across societies and industry is an echo from previous moments of economic calamity and points to a cycle where technology advances new ways to thrive. Ron Epperson was Ernst & Young's Head of Intellectual Property Consulting, specifically working with clean energy tech. He was one of the trailblazers leveraging technologies to affect sustainability before the rise of ESG in the corporate landscape. "After the 2008 financial crisis," Epperson said, "I had an opportunity to lean into the clean tech industry and startup world ... primarily in energy development."

"One of them," Epperson said, "was developing and building renewable energy projects. We were bringing those kinds of technologies and capabilities to First Nations people who really understood sustainability and protecting the environment, probably more than anybody else on the planet."

Epperson transitioned his experience to work in strategic partner initiatives at Texas State University, where he gets involved in such areas as deploying smart city or connected infrastructure technologies and creating platforms for companies to come together and collaborate with the university and each other to figure out interoperability issues and demonstrate technologies. He pointed out how these things sometimes run in cycles, but ultimately emerging technologies only stick if they make money. "When I went to school a long time ago," Epperson said, "I studied what was called alternative energy during the Carter administration. That's the first wave of solar and wind, geothermal and electric vehicles. We were working on that stuff in the '70s."

But, Epperson said, "For most of my career, oil was really cheap. And because oil is really cheap, none of these technologies were more than niche players. Remember, in the 2000s, we had a big run-up in energy prices, and suddenly it made a lot of these technologies economically viable."

Epperson continued,

> In commercializing new products, if you're substituting for an existing product, not only do you have to be better, you have to be cheaper and better. Otherwise, there's no incentive to make the move. So, as we develop these new technologies, approaches, business models, and use cases, we have to think, how can I do it more sustainably and cheaper? Because that's what makes it stick.

The conversation with Epperson highlighted another aspect of what happened during the pandemic to accelerate sustainability: sustainability was and increasingly is less of a "cost center" and more a matter of risk— risk to brand, risk of non-compliance, risk of employee engagement and more. We examine this further in the chapter dedicated to the role of the business sector in this book.

Jason Vazzano, CEO and cofounder of NTT's Vectorform , has dedicated his career to the convergence of emerging technology with societal and business innovation. "I've always been a technology enthusiast and entrepreneur for almost all my life, and I love the transformational change that technology can enable. It is such a superpower for all that choose to wield it."

Vectorform is a 22-year-old innovation company which, Vazzano noted, "predominately supports Fortune 500 organizations and helps them create a culture of courage. They themselves can essentially experiment and try new things with the aim of driving growth and transformational change."

Vazzano elaborated. "It's great to bring many people together to work on exciting projects and try and experiment," but he further urged, "We really need to advocate not for where industries are today … but where these industries are going tomorrow, and how to be the experts in those fields." As software and hardware connect the dots across industries, Vazanno also noted, "We see the intersection of industries really being probably the most exciting opportunity for change, for innovation." Perhaps in the same way that the pandemic brought people closer together through digital innovation, we are in a hallmark moment in history where digitalization can help enterprises across industry work more closely together toward new innovative breakthroughs in the name of collective progress.

Steve Ramseur, the former Chief Innovation Officer of JLL, approached the facets of technology's surge and relationship with sustainability from a property technology (prop-tech) angle. "We moved into the prop-tech space almost eleven years ago. There will be about USD$21B of investment in prop tech this year. We've looked at 900 different prop-tech companies, invested in 31 prop-tech companies, and purchased five." That experience, Ramseur said, allowed them to accelerate during the pandemic, because of the greater awareness and consciousness toward sustainability throughout the lockdowns. "The prop-tech I launched in March of 2020," Ramseur said, "allowed our professionals to virtually do real estate."

What I mean is that 90% of corporate occupiers expect a virtual tour before they step foot inside of a space. So now let's translate that to sustainability. Think about the fact that buildings emit somewhere between 30 to 35% of all greenhouse gas emissions in the world. If we can bring the sustainability conversation to the front and not to the back and enable our clients to use technology to go beyond LEED certification or smart green building or EnergyStar—to go beyond all of that—we can have the conversation.

"Imagine," Ramseur prompted,

> you're a corporate occupier looking for a full floor in Austin, Texas. If I can have the conversation with you ahead of time around employees, commuting, work, modalities, and all those types of different issues, then we can talk about the buildings that have lower carbon footprints. Then I can use a model to put in front of you a dashboard, so as you're selecting buildings in Austin, you're able to not only look at rental rate, fit out, free rent, and all the real estate metrics, you're also able to look at all of the carbon metrics, and you're able to look at all of the human metrics. Now you have a holistic picture of what you're doing with your footprint.

Ramseur said this is a tremendous change from pre-pandemic. Customers have embraced this "unequivocally—in every single conversation." Pre-pandemic, he said, it was nice to have, and might have been a factor. "For example," he said,

> if I'm selecting space in Austin and I'm looking at the domain, I'm looking at downtown, I'm looking different areas. I would have taken these factors into consideration three or four years ago, but they weren't going to be in my top three. Today, they *are* the top three. How are my employees going to work? How am I impacting my community environment?

Those are the top characteristics. It's no longer rental rate. Ramseur notes that while economics are obviously important, they're no longer everything.

More Tech in Our Lives—for Better or for Worse

Vito Mabrucco, Chief Marketing Officer at NTT, saw the advancing role of digitalization as a double-edged sword, and an opportunity for us to rethink our choices. As he put it,

> COVID helped us understand that our health and well-being and our ability to survive in this world are very interdependent on each other. So, I think there's an acceleration in the thinking—we never thought of [traveling from one place to another] as being a risky proposition. But COVID introduced the fact that people getting on planes and traveling around the world created a pandemic through no fault of their own. The interdependence in

this idea (that we can cause great harm or great good when we do things together) is a notion that I think COVID helped to accelerate.

He continued to say that in addition to the impact of and to human interaction during the pandemic, technology became indispensable. Mabrucco explained, "Layer onto that technology, and how technology can help either accelerate that or make it worse. In this case, it's done both; we've become even more dependent on technology." He noted that the isolation of the pandemic may have made us more vulnerable to misinformation, even as we were more aware of other information (such as the murder of George Floyd, for instance, which served as a flashpoint for so many communities around the world).

Mabrucco pulled through the sustainability thread in our discussion:

> I believe we should look at technology and ask, how is it going to contribute to sustainability? I've always believed that technology can help us solve the problems that we have. Today's innovations in technology, help us move ahead. As long as we understand the potential pitfalls that it can create, it can be better for us all. I think that's where we are with technology and sustainability. It can do a lot of good for us, whether it's digital twins or AI or blockchain. These can help us achieve more equality, more equitable prosperity around the world, and more access to health and education and healthcare. Technology can do all that.

But Mabrucco further cautioned,

> "If we can recognize that we can use the technology to help solve some of our basic human challenges, we'll be a lot better off in how we manage the big potential side effects and the potential bad outcomes. It's a different problem, and that's going to require a level of collaboration or level of connectedness around the world, around governments and organizations, to prevent a (sustainability) disaster.

Similar sentiments were shared by Mani Balakrishnan as he debated the merits of our saturation with digital technologies. Balakrishnan called out Albert Einstein, who "was a great scientist, but he tried to do something good for the society, but he was really conscious about how science could be used in a bad way." He described how Einstein was also a celebrated humanist, writing on topics on social science in addition to the great works on technological science.

Mabrucco then said something that became an even more popular sentiment with the popular release of ChatGPT 4: "AI could be the end of humanity. If we're not careful how AI is implemented, it could be the end of us, right?" We dive deeper into AI later in this chapter.

Ben Way, the founder of Freetricity, described how technology innovation toward sustainable outcomes has been a constant throughout his career. "This may be a bit macabre," he said,

> but I've always thought from a very young age, probably from age five or six, that our world was unsustainable at a fundamental level. I've always kind of seen it, the way we live our lives, particularly in the last ten years as the wealth gap has gotten worse. We must change; otherwise, it will collapse. So there has always been in my thought process: Is there any technology that's going to save us one way or another? I've always been very passionate about trying to build those technologies that would save us from collapse.

Way also pointed to how technology can create new problems.

> I've always thought that technology would bring us closer together, free us in a way that nothing else could. But what seems to have happened is that technology has started to erode what it is to be human, or the human experience, and it has tribalized us.

Way continued,

> I think this causes us to make worse decisions, because technology—by its very definition, by doing so much for us—has made us less good at analytical thinking and problem-solving. We tend to focus on short-term solutions rather than long-term solutions.

To Way's observation, while technology has largely been our friend, perhaps it has made us lazy. Perhaps the Great Digitalization during the pandemic has made us more than ever reliant on digitalization and technology, in a way that may not serve us well. Perhaps the pandemic is a canary in the coal mine—an early warning about how systemic societal structures are beginning to collapse. "For the first time," Way noted, people are realizing

> this is not business as usual. Governments move very slowly, and even though they've been moving faster in the environmental and social space,

what we're going to see in the next ten years will pale in comparison to anything we've experienced. This current phase of Western civilization has lasted approximately 300 years, and every great society generally, in human terms, has lasted between 250 and 325 years.

"A belief I've always had," Way added,

> is that, as a society, it's just a basic energy problem. Entropy. You know, as a system grows and gets more complex, its efficiency declines substantially. So, you know, the burden on the end human becomes greater and greater the more sophisticated a society is. Ultimately, it becomes less efficient. And that burden is then placed in terms of tax or management on the kind of end user.

Way warned, "Once that burden is too great, then, of course, we get social unrest and the collapse of that civilization."

The overall tenor of our conversation was optimistic, though. "While I still have great hope," he said,

> there are really two paths out of this. One is a technical path where technology does save us—it's that great thing, the threading a camel through the eye of a needle. Or, once we do have a great reset, what grows out of it is far fairer on humanity than today's world.

Technology Trade-Offs

Carla Bailo approached technology's pros and cons indirectly, through the lens of her background in polymeric materials. Now President and CEO of the Center for Automotive Research, as well as on the board of SM Energy and Advanced Auto Parts, she has seen a lot of changes in the automotive industry and recalled experiences in encountering both the positive and negative impacts of innovation—by technology or science or both. "I love chemistry and polymers," she said,

> but when we were studying them, we didn't realize that they never went away. That's kind of the root of my adventure and my thoughts about sustainability: the fact that we created some really great stuff, it's really convenient, but it's now causing a lot of problems with the environment, and it's

made from oil. Things that we didn't think about when we were working on this. It was the new future, right?

Bailo brought those same pro-con dynamic considerations to her experience at the intersection of mobility and the automotive industry. "In the automotive industry, we're all worried about profits and the number of vehicles and volumes," she said, which contrasted with her view on how to think of the utility of vehicles as an enabler of mobility. "The thing that really changed my mind about mobility was when I led the Columbus Smart City Project," Bailo continued,

> That was all about how mobility can provide ladders of opportunity for jobs, for education, for health care. We focused on a particular neighborhood that had four times the national average of infant mortality—in many cases related to an inability to get good health care during pregnancy and after birth. So we really focused on these communities and getting out and talking to people about their struggles with mobility. They're not even talking about owning a car. They just needed a cheap way to get around, and owning a car was something they never even envisioned they'd be able to do. This completely changed my thinking about the mobility ecosystem.

During the pandemic, there were no vehicles, no transportation to anywhere. Which for a lot of people was a bonus to "saving the Earth" from dangerous GHG emissions. While embraced by many, this severely impacted the ability of some individuals and families to fundamentally live—to buy groceries, get healthcare, and earn a living.

Planes, Trains, and New Technologies

Public transit and transportation systems were heavily impacted from the very onset of the pandemic. In the United States, according to the American Public Transportation Association, public ridership dropped to 80% of 2019 levels in April 2020 and stayed at around 60% of 2019 levels for the remainder of the year.[9] Meanwhile, the "essential worker" workforce relied heavily on public transportation systems to get to work and other basic needs. As we all became sensitized to the impact that transportation emissions have on the environment, transportation agencies in communities, in turn, focused on sustainable alternatives to be ready for when the industry resumed a new post-pandemic normal. The US Department of Transportation estimated that the US transportation sector alone accounted for 33% of GHG emissions in the United States. Accordingly, during the pandemic, the United States released an updated Climate Action Plan, prioritizing key areas of focus:

- Incorporate Resilience into DOT Grant and Loan Programs.
- Enhance Resilience Throughout the Project Planning and Development Process.
- Ensure Resiliency of DOT Facilities and Operational Assets.
- Ensure Climate-ready Services and Supplies.
- Improve Climate Education and Research on Resilience.[10]

On the other side of the pond, in a three-decade span report culminating in the year of the pandemic, 2020, the European Union (EU) observed the transportation sector as being the only sector that saw in increase in emissions (see Figure 1.2).[11]

When the world emerged from COVID-19 restrictions, CO_2 emissions jumped 8% in 2021, from 2020. To get to net zero emissions by 2050, CO_2 emissions from the sector must fall by about 3% per year to 2030. The EU alone is targeting 2030 zero-emissions for new city buses and 90% emissions reductions for new trucks by 2040 with its Green New Deal.[12] These ambitions need funding, regulation, and innovative technologies and new breakthroughs in infrastructure.

When we spoke with Steve Young, Vice President of Tech & Innovation for San Antonio Transit, he shared specific insights from the public transportation sector. Metro transit is not an area many people think of when they consider sustainability measures but, as Young noted, transit fulfills many purposes. Education and transportation are two of the most vital sectors to society—without education and/or transportation, ways to pursue economic means are scarce.

San Antonio Transit has an 800-vehicle bus fleet burning fossil fuels, which Young notes limits the number of vehicles on the road. Even a bus with only ten passengers is better than ten cars on the road, for instance. No single-occupant vehicle will be as efficient as a large vehicle with a dense population. As a result, Young said, transit is one of the keys to a sustainable future, especially in cities.

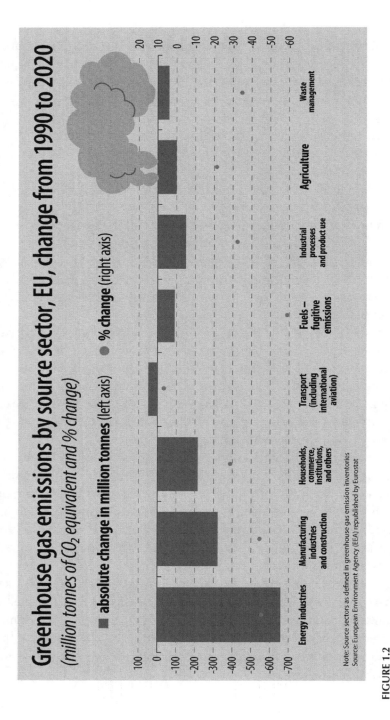

FIGURE 1.2

Changes in Greenhouse Gas (GHG) emissions by source sector in Europe—between 1990 and 2020

Young pointed to how layers of bureaucracy affect the sustainability measures an organization can make. In the case of San Antonio Transit, he said, "We're governed by an appointed board [with] appointees from the city, the county, and some of the other suburban cities." He noted that while the board is very focused on how they can work to create a greener environment, a greener fleet, the fact remains they have to work with the infrastructure in place.

For San Antonio Transit, that may not mean electric vehicles are the best solution. "There's a lot of challenges with electrification," Young said,

> We did a couple of generation-one vehicles for buses, and they're pretty much research vehicles. There's no way we could ever put them in service on a big suburban route. No one factored in the number of miles and then the heat load in San Antonio. Yes, this bus can go 100 miles, but once you turn the air conditioner on, it can only go ten. So that's a factor for San Antonio.

Instead, Young said, they were able to make great strides with natural gas. "I think a lot of people don't appreciate it because it's not electric," Young said, but "we run a huge number of natural gas buses, one of the largest fleets in the United States. Compared to diesel, the amount of pollution these buses make is just phenomenally less." Young estimated this may be as much as an 80–90% reduction in nasty pollutants, plus "it happens to be leveraging a fuel that is in natural abundance in South Texas, so it works out really well in a lot of ways."

"Of course," Young continued, "the problem with a lot of green technologies is that all of a sudden, traditional infrastructure doesn't support them. And that was the problem for us converting to compressed natural gas (CNG)." San Antonio didn't have the infrastructure—so they built it. At the time, Young said, "it was North America's largest compressed natural gas facility, on-site here in San Antonio—just to have the power to bring in that much fuel, where it's got to be compressed and pumped into so many vehicles every night."

Red, No, Blue—No, Green!

Given the surge in digital content, social media grew commensurately in power and prominence to influence how people think and why they would think the way they do. So not surprisingly, sustainability became a more politicized agenda thanks to:

1. Echo Chambers: Social media platforms tend to create echo chambers, where users are exposed to content that aligns with their existing beliefs and values. This reinforces existing opinions and can lead to the formation of polarized communities. In the case of sustainability, individuals with different political leanings may gravitate toward specific online communities that either support or reject sustainability efforts, which could lead to unmerited conflicting agendas.

2. Disinformation and Misinformation: Social media platforms have been susceptible to the spread of disinformation and misinformation. People or groups with specific agendas may intentionally distort facts or manipulate data to undermine sustainability initiatives or promote alternative viewpoints. This can create confusion and skepticism among users, making it difficult to establish consensus or gain widespread support for sustainability goals.

3. Amplification of Extremes: Social media platforms often amplify extreme viewpoints. This can lead to an oversimplification of complex sustainability issues, where nuanced discussions are overshadowed by extreme positions. As a result, moderate voices and pragmatic solutions may struggle to gain visibility, contributing to the politicization of the sustainability agenda.

4. Tribalism and Identity Politics: Social media platforms encourage the formation of online tribes based on shared beliefs and identities. Sustainability, with its multidimensional nature and interconnectedness to various societal issues, can become entangled with existing political ideologies and identity politics. As a result, sustainability efforts may be seen as aligned with a particular political group, leading to a partisan approach and the politicization of the agenda.

5. Influencer Culture and Branding: Social media influencers play a significant role in shaping public opinion. However, their endorsements or critiques of sustainability initiatives may be driven by personal or financial interests rather than a genuine commitment to the cause. The influencer culture can create a perception that sustainability is driven by commercial motives or specific political affiliations, further politicizing the issue.

Despite the challenges, overall digital media saturations have raised awareness more so, fostered dialogue, and mobilized communities toward positive change.

Andreas Sjostrom, Vice President and Director of Applied Innovation Exchange at Capgemini, talked about the role that information and access provided to influence social sustainability "I know that the topic of sustainability and responsible innovation is wider than climate change," Sjostrom said, "but I am always very focused on my listening ears. I'm tuning in to those who widen the term with the purpose of directing the attention away from climate change, instead of what makes that person look good." He continued with his holistic approach to sustainability. If he hears someone say something along the lines of, "Let's focus on the ethics in AI. Let's not think about greenhouse gas emissions," Sjostrom said, "I am listening carefully every time that happens." There are context clues, Sjostrom noted. "I'm figuring out first, actually, are you in a red state or a blue state? What kind of labor do you have? Do you believe in climate change science?"

All that aside, Sjostrom said, "I'm very happy. 2021 was a record-breaking year from a climate tech perspective. The State of California itself initiated and ignited hundreds of exciting new climate tech startups in transportation logistics, in energy power, and in agriculture and food." Sjostrom gave context. "The $25 billion into climate-change-related funds was record-breaking. It went from $4 billion in 2017 to $25 billion in 2021. It's just a tremendous impact." Sjostrom added, "I see exciting companies in the hydrogen infrastructure play," Sjostrom mused. "I see interesting plays in AI, machine learning, material science, and so on. Across the board, we have entrepreneurs and innovators taking this super-seriously, VCs are only investing in startups with a purpose-driven investment strategy."

"So," Sjostrom said,

I am coming back to being realistic, but also being very much a techno-optimist. I believe in the good in people and that we will eventually solve all of this. But it's going to take time, and it's going to take a lot of energy on all levels, from business to politicians and regulations, and all of that.

The impact of social media on the sustainability agenda is multifaceted, and we should maintain vigilance to ensure the dissemination of accurate information and constructive discussions.

"Heavy Mental"

As sustainability becomes increasingly integrated into our collective human experience and industries, we typically associate it with climate action, energy efficiency, Diversity, Equity, and Inclusion (DEI), social justice, biodiversity, and more. However, during interviews conducted, an unexpected but critical aspect of sustainability emerged—mental health.

Amidst the interviews, it became evident that mental health is a topic often overlooked in sustainability discussions. The pandemic, in all its "Black Swan" characteristics, has inflicted widespread stress on our generation. Its impact has been felt universally, leading to a deterioration of physical and mental well-being, loss of lives, instances of domestic violence, job and income loss, and disruptions of varying degrees in our daily lives. These experiences have caused immense mental anguish across all age groups in our societies. According to an article from the Kaiser Family Foundation, "Rise in Use of Mental Health Apps Raises New Policy Issues," digital behavioral health services such as mental health apps became distinctly more popular during the pandemic. In the United States, about 40% of the population reported symptoms of anxiety or depression in 2020, and the funding of behavioral health startups boomed during the pandemic with US$588 million invested in the first half of the same year.[13]

It is imperative to recognize mental health as an integral component of sustainability, as it directly affects our ability to sustain ourselves as a society. Addressing mental health challenges is not only crucial for individual well-being but also for fostering resilient communities and building a sustainable future. By acknowledging and incorporating mental health considerations into sustainability forums, we can cultivate a more holistic and inclusive approach to our collective well-being.

Naoko Okumoto is the founder and managing director of the NIREMIA Collective, an early-stage fund specializing in well-being tech. She observed that the feeling of not belonging has become altogether too common in all too many settings—and that is something the NIREMIA Collective is addressing with the projects it helps fund. Little wonder that the digital behavioral health market is booming. In some ways, this mental anguish, and a fundamental questioning of the "what is my purpose" in the face of death and disease was a large factor in the quiet-quitting phenomenon mentioned earlier. Okumoto noted that at least one survey of Gen Z found that 80% said their well-being was most important, more so even than money. The pandemic created a seismic shift in a sense of self-awareness and a search for answers online.

The silver lining in the saga of mental anguish is that three years of the pandemic made us more human with an unprecedented and shared experience. As Okumoto shared, the pandemic increased a sense of shared humanity which, in turn, allowed others to be vulnerable and helped people create better relationships, which in turn, support mental health and well-being.

Remembering Our Humanity

It can be easy to get carried away with virtualization, digitalization, metrics, and data. Baiju Shah, Chief Strategy Officer of Accenture Song, and Head of Growth and Strategy at Accenture, reminded us of the importance of being grounded in the humanity of our existence.

Shah shared that Accenture Song was first called Accenture Interactive, but the name changed as part of "a massive rebrand, as a signal towards increasing humanity. As it turns out, even though there's a lot of technology possible, we strongly believe that we need to over-index on the people side."

Shah explained that a background in computer science helped him start his career. "I was looking at technology innovation, thinking about the unlimited technology possibility. Of course, I learned you can do anything with technology; that was never the constraint." Instead, Shah challenged, "The constraint is what should you do and what will businesses and users take on?" He went back to business school, reshaping his "career in business innovation, trying to understand how to connect big, bold ideas, knowing that you can do anything with technology to business." In that sense, Accenture Interactive, Shah said, was built on the third leg of the stool, "which was the human side, understanding human need."

"There's a whole bunch of reasons why," he said,

> but I firmly believe that you need all three of these lenses to do things that are sustainable and to drive sustained value to both people and the planet. That's my overall thesis: the requirement of being these hybrid innovators is to understand the consequences to all different dimensions.

Ultimately, the pandemic initiated a pondering of how we, as a global community, were going to align on containing and combating the virus.

And, at the same time, it was a period of existential angst for how we were going to recognize our common experience and use this to catalyze us forward as a collective, global community.

Artificial Intelligence: Villain or Superhero?

The pandemic was, in so many ways, a time when we became heavily reliant on technology and the respective digitalization, as software, hardware, and data converged. And while devices and applications have largely helped us be resilient and thrive through one of the most catastrophic times in our human history, we should also maintain a larger perspective—looking at the consequences of new technologies, who those technologies benefit, and how those technologies can be made inclusive—of the ways advanced digitalization is to our benefit, or our detriment, especially with respect to AI.

One of the leading voices in the application of AI to the human existence, Sagie Davidovich, CEO of SparkBeyond, shared his perspectives, anchored by many years working with one of the most popular AI mechanisms to date—ChatGPT. His team at SparkBeyond has built an automated research engine, capable of asking questions and discovering complex patterns in data, with these patterns serving as powerful tools for explaining, predicting, and optimizing outcomes. As he explained, "Generative is not a new concept, but there seems to be a consensus that it has reached an escape velocity and it's good enough to be ready for the masses and undisputedly create value." Davidovich continued,

> Let's explore this. One angle is negative. Large language models (LLMs) can be extremely energy hungry. In addition, you need to multiply the amount of energy that's required to train and use them by the number of users. We also brought them to the masses. I know that Microsoft is already building around 80 gigawatt of data centers, just for generative AI—and there are at least hundreds of data centers just for this AI pursuit. But there is also a positive angle to the relationship between generative AI and sustainability. It's a super brain to whom we can ask questions. With it, we can use humanity's collective intelligence to help us with one of the greatest challenges of this generation. We might have a better chance.
>
> It's not just like in *The Hitchhiker's Guide to the Galaxy*, where you can just give it a single command for a single answer, such as "tell me how to solve climate." It's much more nuanced and granular. It's probably millions

of questions that companies in their own local context need to ask about the materials that they use. Can they be replaced with more sustainable alternatives? How can waste products be repurposed to use to be recycled or upcycled right to an increased circularity? How can entire processes be eliminated or merged in order to drive additional efficiency? Multiple expert consultancies do these things today, but they are not democratized and it's expensive. There are still too many of them and too few of them at the same time. Here, suddenly, we have something that costs at most $20 a month and can answer questions when it has access to literally the entire web.

AI as a concept or mechanism is not new—the term was first coined in the 1950s. It has continued to proliferate in usage and capabilities, particularly with the explosion of data from digitalization. The recent fervor over ChatGPT has brought the terminology to the mainframe of business, government, community, education, and probably every aspect of who we are and how we live. AI in and of itself is not going to be the superhero that eliminates the villains in sustainability, but it can and, hopefully, will give us humans the superpower of credible and objective scenario planning and predictive resource management and maintenance.

We can anticipate that AI will augment our own intelligence. As Davidovich puts it,

> A fascinating cross-pollination is happening. I think that this is maybe one of the most exciting decades in which to live, because we see the cross-pollination between neuroscience and artificial intelligence like never before. We use AI to investigate brains in Japan. A group of researchers there demonstrated the very capable system that used deep neural networks that can read one's mind and thoughts and visualize them.

Davidovich continued,

> This sounds like science fiction material, but if you think about it, it's not very different than any other sort of signal processing. You just need to learn how to decipher what's happening. And that's one thing that it's good at. But then the other angle is we learn from the topology of neural pathways about architectures that can inspire—biomimicry that can inspire future architectures of deep neural networks.

Ultimately, the responsibility is heavier on humans than ever before. With the technology tools and innovation best practices that continue to proliferate, we have an unprecedented opportunity to achieve breakthroughs in addressing these critical challenges.

Problem Solved—But at Scale?

Xavier Denoly is Corporate Sustainability Officer for Schneider Electric. His view of the role of utilities in building a sustainable future was similarly utilitarian. Schneider Electric was founded in 1836 as a steel manufacturer, eventually evolving to weapons manufacturing, then delving into electric switches. Today, Schneider is a leading digital automation and electric management enterprise. For Denoly, that starts with data, and advances with scale. He observed that "Increasingly over the past 10 or 15 years, what has happened is with the rise of digital technology, we have leveraged digital technology, to be able to capture, if you want, the state of every single installation that uses electrical energy." Combing that data, Denoly said, "allows for predictive maintenance, for simulation, to allow for all these good things we have today with the combination of digital and software to make the infrastructure at an optimal stage."

Data is one leg of the stool, Denoly explained. Second is reduced consumption—often by "going even deeper using the latest technologies to have the best electrical energy efficiency." The third is "to organize the switch as much as possible to renewable types of energies." To Denoly's mind, we do a disservice by not appreciating the technologies we already have. "A lot of people place a lot of hope on innovation, which I think is good," he said, "but we just have to be careful not to bet our collective future on hypothetical technical innovation that might come someday." Denoly continued, "We have most of the technology already existing today to be able to very significantly curb the problem. The problem is scaling."

Denoly used housing as an example, noting that most of the housing and buildings we'll use in the future are already built. "The problem is how do we upgrade all the existing buildings and facilities that we already have, so that these buildings or houses or apartment blocks become positive in terms of energy? That's a simple one on paper. But to me, it really takes the authorities," he said, and a "need to make it compulsory. We need to subsidize, to help fund the transformation so that we can transform the building sector over time." He continued, "It's possible the technologies we need to be able to do that already exist," Denoly recommended

Get rid of all the heaters in the house that are powered by fuel or by gas or by a coal mine. This should be prohibited in some way, and then the replacement equipment already exists ... It's called heat pumps, or it's called electric heaters, but that works only if the electrical network is decarbonized.

As Denoly illustrated, the problem is one of scale:

If you want to push people to switch to electric vehicles, pushing people to switch to lots of things powered by electricity, but at the same time, we continue to produce our own electricity with coal power plants with all these fuel power plants, we are just shifting the problem. We are not solving anything.

While sustainability challenges like climate change call for urgency of action, it is unrealistic to expect immediate and complete transformation. Rushing toward existing solutions without careful consideration may lead to temporary fixes. It is crucial to be cautious about making trade-offs when adopting a solution to solve a problem. Instead, we should utilize the technology that is presently accessible to make necessary changes wherever possible, and gradually incorporate new technologies as they become viable. Rather than relying solely on future technologies to rescue us, we must take incremental steps toward improvement.

Small Steps over No Steps, Every Day, and Every Way

Incremental progress plays a significant role in achieving larger goals. Each step in the evolutionary process represents a continuous improvement built upon the lessons learned from the preceding ones. This concept, popularized by the Japanese automotive industry with the term "kaizen"" (改善), emphasizes the importance of constant refinement. Youngcho Chi, Executive Vice President at Hyundai, has witnessed significant changes in the automotive sector. When Chi joined Hyundai, like other major car manufacturers, there was little emphasis on aspects such as ESG factors. However, with brands like Tesla capturing the attention of the general public and raising awareness about electric vehicles, coupled with a growing recognition of the environmental impact of fossil fuel-powered cars, the industry's focus has dramatically shifted—but change still needs to be through diligent step changes. Chi highlighted his recent endeavors in areas like Connectivity, Autonomous mobility, Service, and Electrification (CASE) as a testament to this transformed process.

"A lot of this is really about the environment," Chi said, "about putting humans at the center, not the technology at the center. Is it better to own a car, or is it better to actually share a car? So I think all of that." He pointed to how he used to travel so regularly for work that it was only during the pandemic lockdown—when he could not travel—that he realized how many of his trips would have worked just as well digitally, without the travel. "I came to the realization that a lot of the trips I made prior to 2019, I didn't have to travel," Chi admitted. "Of course, it's wrong to go extreme and say no more travel—all business is going to be done digitally or virtually. That's going too extreme." But Chi travels much less frequently, making things more manageable all around. That is a technology choice that already exists.

Serial entrepreneur Ivo Timoteo, founder and CEO of Braid Industries, a venture-backed startup that harnesses scientific tools and ideas to develop best-performing designs across industries, observed how technology companies had to shift their path to growth. Economically, he said, "It's definitely not like the previous 20–30 years whereby doing nothing you would grow." The shift is that you no longer grow by doing nothing. Instead, he said, "It forces you to be much more honest as a company, and it forces you to be much more honest in your work." Timoteo noted the pandemic "removed the possibility of faking it for too much longer," because a population that is more active on social media is also more aware of what is going on in the world around them, which in turn creates that change movement and an expectation that corporations do better.

"Too many technology startups try to solve an incredibly hard problem by picking the flashiest problem to solve first, and that's not usually how good problems are solved," Timoteo noted.

> But pick something simple and create a concrete value and then keep expanding on that simple thing and it's not a bad thing. If every single step of your company is a simple step that you can enact in six months, people will love to work there because you always have positive reinforcement and positive feedback.

That should be a frame for all organizations, not just technology companies. Give your people reasons to be hopeful, encouraged, and invested. Small steps are better than none, and never have those small steps been so important.

Technology and Sustainability—Two Sides of the Post-Pandemic Coin

The Great Digitalization that was accelerated by the pandemic played multiple roles in the ways that sustainability and ESG were intensified during the pandemic. This intensification has repercussions in the post-COVID world to which we are adjusting. On May 5, 2023, the World Health Organization officially declared that the pandemic was over, which is a relief, for sure. But we now need to determine how we "knit" together all the ways that data, connectivity, and intelligence are redefining our existence—and more profoundly, the extension of our existence past the climate change crisis that unfolds and regularly precipitates in new ways.

The plodding toward "net zero" and "carbon zero" we see in the industry will not meaningfully move us toward the outcomes committed to by so many organizations with 2030, 2040, and 2050 dates. To make substantial advancements, we require a widespread and accelerated adoption of emerging technologies and digitalization. This convergence, which was accelerated during the pandemic, has greatly enhanced our capacity to measure, analyze, improve, and innovate upon crucial targets and key performance indicators (KPIs). It is crucial in breaking through to new energy paradigms, fostering circular economy practices, preserving biodiversity, and promoting social and gender equity. This transformative leap may come in the form of new AI technologies.

While the large language models found in AI tools like ChatGPT are dominating the headlines right now, as we approach the second half of this 20s decade, we are on the brink of new ways that intelligent algorithms will help us problem-solve some of humanity's greatest challenges. And it will take the collective focus and effort of communities, business, governance/government, and financial firepower for us to preserve our life in and around our global neighborhoods. We dive into those factors here next.

NOTES

1. We Are Social. [n.d]. *Digital 2020 US: Your Ultimate Guide to the Digital Evolving World*. Retrieved November 1, 2023 from https://wearesocial.com/us/blog/2020/01/digital-2020-us/
2. Molla, R. (2020, December 4). *The Pandemic Was Great for Zoom: What Happens When There's a Vaccine?* Vox. https://www.vox.com/recode/21726260/zoom-micro-soft-teams-video-conferencing-post-pandemic-coronavirus

3. Nicas, J. (2020, August 19). Apple reaches $2 trillion, punctuating big tech's grip. *The New York Times.* https://www.nytimes.com/2020/08/19/technology/apple-2 -trillion.html

4. Shankland, S. (2023, June 1). *The Man Who Named the Metaverse Is Optimistic Despite Waning Hype.* CNET. https://www.cnet.com/tech/gaming/the-man-who -named-the-metaverse-is-optimistic-despite-waning-hype/

5. United Nations. Department of Economic and Social Affairs. Retrieved May 10, 2022 from https://sdgs.un.org/goals.

6. Butterfly Effect. (2023, March 29). In Wikipedia. https://en.wikipedia.org/wiki/ Butterfly_effect.

7. Hamed, M. (2022, February 8). *2021-2023 Emerging Technology Roadmap for Large Enterprises.* LinkedIn. https://www.linkedin.com/pulse/2021-2023-emerging -technology-roadmap-large-mohamed-hamed/

8. Xue, Y. (2021, December 21). Why data centres, 5G networks are at the forefront of climate-change fight in China. *South China Morning Post.* https://www.scmp.com /business/article/3161075/why-data-centres-5g-networks-are-forefront-climate -change-fight-china

9. EBP US, Inc. (2021). *The Impact of the COVID-19 Pandemic on Public Transit Funding Needs in the U.S.* American Public Transportation Association. https:// www.apta.com/wp-content/uploads/APTA-COVID-19-Funding-Impact-2021-01 -27.pdf

10. U.S Department of Transportation. Climate action. Retrieved March 29, 2023 from https://www.transportation.gov/priorities/climate-and-sustainability/climate -action.

11. Eurostat. (2022). *Greenhouse Gas Emissions by Source Sector, EU, Change from 1990 to 2020.* Image. European Union. https://ec.europa.eu/eurostat/web/products -eurostat-news/-/ddn-20220823-1

12. European Union. (2023, February 14). *European Green Deal: Commission Proposes 2030 Zero-Emissions Target for New City Buses and 90% Emissions Reductions for New Rucks by 2040* [Press Release]. https://ec.europa.eu/commission/presscorner/ detail/en/IP_23_762

13. Panchal, N., Saunders, H., Rudowitz, R., & Cox, C. (2023). *The Implications of Covid-19 for Mental Health and Substance Abuse.* KFF. https://www.kff.org/coro- navirus-covid-19/issue-brief/the-implications-of-covid-19-for-mental-health-and -substance-use/

2

Community: Agency and Belonging

BOTTOMS-UP

COVID-19 was a global phenomenon that was unprecedented in its equal opportunity impact. Never before in human history has every nation, every community, every family, and every individual endured the kind of common experience catalyzed by the health crisis, retail panic (toilet paper still seems too expensive), and universal shut-out and shut-in. In particular, the lockdown created the environment that would facilitate a movement that is a cornerstone to the "Social" in Environmental, Social, and Governance (ESG)—the social aspects of Diversity, Equity, and Inclusion (DEI).

How Did This Happen?

Let's start by examining the dynamics of movements and the mechanisms that drive them forward. An example that might be immediately familiar is President Barack Obama's first presidential campaign. As an outsider and relative unknown, Obama was still in his first term in the US Senate when he ran for President of the United States. Obama's campaign relied heavily on local organizing, utilizing many of the same grassroots tactics he had used in his experience as a grassroots community organizer, and he became an early innovator in using the power of social media.

Some of the ways in which the Obama campaign made use of community movement principles included:

DOI: 10.4324/9781003462347-2

- A campaign slogan ("Yes, we can") that borrowed directly from a long history of union organizing and other community movements.
- Leveraging social media—particularly compared to how little this had been used by most previous political campaigns. The year Obama came into office, the White House joined Facebook, Twitter, Flickr, Vimeo, and MySpace. In 2105, Obama sent the first tweet from @POTUS.
- Viral videos that extended reach.

Other politicians since have, of course, built on the lessons of Obama's first presidential campaign. What is most telling for the context of this book, however, is how this model leveraged the reach and influence of digital channels in developing more widespread support and driving responsive action for community change.

Similar mechanisms have galvanized several community-driven, bottom-up movements throughout the course of modern history. The Black Lives Matter movement pre-dated COVID but leveraged similar mechanics to reach a new crescendo during the pandemic. It all culminated through the motions of a captive audience to digital media streams, COVID-related stress and anxiety that could further fuel emotional sparks, broader adoption of social media as a communication medium, and business interests in appealing to diverse communities in the war for talent. However, a salient ingredient in this perfect storm was the tragic murder of George Floyd so viscerally captured on video and audio.

When this tragedy occurred during the early days of the pandemic, most of us were trapped indoors, working from home, or furloughed, as only essential workers were mobilized. The images and audio of the video spread like wildfire to all corners of the world. And they galvanized us in ways that "#BlackLivesMatter" had not been able to do before. For many, it was impossible to see the video and not feel like something had to be done. The Floyd tragedy, and the #BlackLivesMatter resurgence then gave fresh life to several related causes—from police accountability to use-of-force laws to policing standards and even prison reform, among others. Floyd's death, combined with other factors related to the pandemic, provided a fresh flashpoint that illuminated the need to focus on social equity and justice. It amplified the sustainability agenda within communities, race relations, and in enterprise talent management.

Mike Burns is a founder of The Burns Brothers, a family of culture-focused companies dedicated to creating a more inclusive world. Soft-spoken yet commanding, Burns brings insights based on his experience as a senior leader in Fortune 500 companies and a former army officer with 13 years of military service. He offered,

> The first thing I'll say is that circumstances tend to be pretty flat. Circumstances in human experience don't drastically change. What drastically changes are what people choose to pay attention to. So, if we're talking specifically about social unrest and some of the injustices were highlighted over the past few years, those injustices—whether it be health and equity, education inequity, or policing—all those things are not new. It's just certain parts of the population chose and had the privilege to not have to pay attention to them.

Burns continued,

> As a Black American, police brutality was not shocking to me. It wasn't something that I first saw with the George Floyd killing. Even as someone who grew up in middle class or upper middle class, I myself have faced that type of situation—obviously not to an extreme—but I've experienced issues with policing. This wasn't new to me.

E. David Ellington echoed the deep sense of déjà vu. Founder and Executive Chairman of the Silicon Valley Blockchain Society (SVBS), as well as a former Trustee and Commissioner on the San Francisco Employees' Retirement System (US$20 billion) Board, Ellington succinctly and tactfully explained, "I think COVID just exposed what we already knew—what people already knew, and have already been living with, and navigating." What was different with George Floyd's death was that people could not easily look away: "It was so ugly and so visual—that video that ran viral of a man saying, 'I can't breathe'." The pandemic catalyzed the emotional outrage and lack of attention to social justice and racial equity—that have been discussed and festering for a very long time.

Stephen Clarke is Senior Director at Jones Lang LaSalle. A dual citizen of the United States and the United Kingdom and the child of Jamaican immigrants to England, he noted that the pandemic restricted movement, and so things were—at least in the early stages—quieter. With that quiet came a greater awareness of the world around us and heightened emotional sensitivity, so Floyd's death was a natural powder keg.

As Clarke emphasized, "We were all home, two months into a global crisis of people's emotion and stress levels, and our hypersensitivity to the crisis was already piqued." He connected this to events that had come earlier: Kobe Bryant had died in a helicopter crash just months before, and the circumstances surrounding his death had reminded people of when Princess Diana had died. People were already talking about tragic deaths. When Floyd's death went viral, Clarke told us, "Once you saw it, you couldn't unsee it." The brutality of those images lingered for him and for many others—and the stress of the lock-down environment likely magnified these experiences.

With societies returning to "normal" and with the obsession with digital media diluting as more time is spent away from screens, we hope that our global society does not turn down the intensity of focus on inequality and injustice again. And with signs and commensurate fears of recession intersecting with the World Health Organization declaring the pandemic "over" in May 2023, the energy and intensity around DEI do seem to be increasingly diluted—especially in the corporate landscape.

As described by Clarke,

> The wind in those sails will die down. Some of it will die down slightly as people try and kickstart the next season of normality or whatever that looks like. I also don't think the pendulum will swing so far back that we're going to lose all of the momentum.

So far that seems to be the case.

#BlackLivesMatter and Broader Social Equity Movements

To be effective and sustainable, movements need renewed winds from community movements to refresh awareness of relevant issues—which is effectively what happened during the pandemic. Studies have examined the ways in which public protests influence public perception and motivate significant action. A Proceedings of the National Academy of Science study released in early 2022[1] found that, "BLM protests dramatically amplify the use of terms associated with the BLM agenda throughout the movement's history," and argued that "these findings indicate that BLM has successfully leveraged protest events to engender lasting changes in the ways that Americans discuss racial inequality."

As Patrisse Cullors—one of the founders of #BlackLivesMatter—argued in a 2020 opinion piece,[2] Black Lives Matter began after Trayvon Martin's death in 2012; Ferguson showed its staying power. For many Americans (especially white Americans), Ferguson was their first key instance of Black Lives Matter and the larger movement for racial equality and an end to police brutality/injustice. Ongoing exposure to Black Lives Matter and a greater understanding of just how often Black men and women were dying led to a greater awareness of police misconduct in the years immediately preceding the pandemic. The graphic video of Floyd was a critical catalyst for broader change—because of the many years that community organizers spent in making us all aware of the issues, and the presence of visceral video footage, à la social media, of Floyd's murder.

Ceah Justice, head of Diversity, Equity, and Inclusion at Raytheon, extrapolated how the digital age can help create access and participation in larger movements. When we discussed the impact that the pandemic had on aspects of sustainability, in this case "social" sustainability, she agreed.

> I think digital played a huge role. Think about what the digital age has done in this time. It has allowed participation from all. So, if you want to participate in some type of movement or understand something beyond your four walls, you're able to do that. I look at that as a positive thing. When we think about allyship, we think about getting more people brought into the causes.

Yvonne Wolf, a global four-time Chief HR Officer (CHRO), Human Capital leader, and Board leader, shared key insights into how organizational culture and human resources can grapple with the issues the pandemic helped bring to the forefront. We started by talking about the perfect storm of Floyd's death. For Wolf, what happened felt like an opportunity for conversations already occurring in some communities to become more widespread. "When everything started happening, I affectionately became the White Male Whisperer. I was happy to have conversations, particularly with white males, about what was happening and how they could help in their journey." But it is also not a surprise to any of us doing the work that Wolf noted those conversations have been emotionally exhausting for her. All too often, people of color are asked to lead the charge when it comes to DEI. Those changes toward a more equitable workplace and society should come from everyone—and requiring a global pandemic to galvanize the efforts. Wolf added, "George Floyd being murdered for everyone to see all over the world just ripped off the Band-Aid—it sort of put everything under a deeper microscope."

Jason Salfi is the co-founder and CEO of startup Dimensional Energy, a solar fuels platform based on novel technology. When we spoke, we both noted how part of the response to George Floyd's death was made possible by the work of Black organizers in previous years. There was an underlying awareness of police brutality against Black people, but the Floyd murder was like pouring oil on a fire, because people were in front of their devices—already in a raw emotional state from COVID and the stresses it was causing—which resulted in much greater access and exposure.

For Salfi, this was the final impetus toward forming an informal working group called White Men for Racial Justice. As Salfi told us, "Our thesis was if white men traditionally have a lot of leverage in society to make change because we do hold primary levers of power, what can we actively do to not repeat the past?" That meant doing more than simply saying, "I'm not one of the bad guys." As Salfi explained, their group had been meeting every Tuesday night:

> We got together to contemplate what is our role in this? What does our inaction do when we don't speak out or we don't act out? What does that mean to the rest of society? Are we in league with the forces that keep the status quo in motion? We've worked together for two years now as a group, and we've started to kind of emerge with actions that, over time, we believe will hopefully gain traction and momentum.

Jen Cohen was CIO at Toyota Research Institute when Floyd died.

> It brought to light an experience that many of us, myself included, don't have, or don't worry about. As a white woman, I have friends who have to have different conversations with their kids, than I've had to have because of the color of their skin, which is insane.

Cohen reflected,

> I think George Floyd really snapped into people's psyche in a way in which nothing, sadly, nothing prior, had. So, during COVID, a lot of conversations

happened. People who weren't exposed to ideas got exposed to this. That marries with a younger generation who's willing to tolerate less ignoring of that, less discussion about that, less inequity.

From Invisible to Visible

Maneesh Sharma is Dean of the College of Business at Embry-Riddle Aeronautical University. He called out other aspects of the pandemic that helped shed light and force us to examine inequities in society. In particular, there was an isolation and a deepening of certain socioeconomic divides.

> You don't hear a CEO getting in a scuffle or getting into a tragic situation with law enforcement, for example. You always hear that the people who are in those kinds of tragic situations are always those who wouldn't be able to work from home.

Sharma continued,

> This has absolutely amplified some of the inequities in our society for humanity as a whole. I know this firsthand from my relatives in India. Those who are the day workers, for example, couldn't work anymore and were not equipped for a "work from home" new world.

The pandemic had a way of putting the inequities in communities and across regions in higher fidelity and with greater amplification. Underserved communities were able to be seen and heard.

More than ever, underserved communities saw the opportunity to make change through the power of digital platforms that proliferated during the pandemic, and to catalyze movement through visual and audio cues of digital media. With technology, the complicated web equity in diversity propagated from communities into the enterprise arena during the pandemic. Following George Floyd's murder, large-scale multinational enterprises activated a commitment to diversity in their workforce. Apple, one of the most powerful technologies on Earth, even changed its homepage (see Figure 2.1)[3] at apple.com to include Black Lives Matter messaging within weeks of the Floyd tragedy.

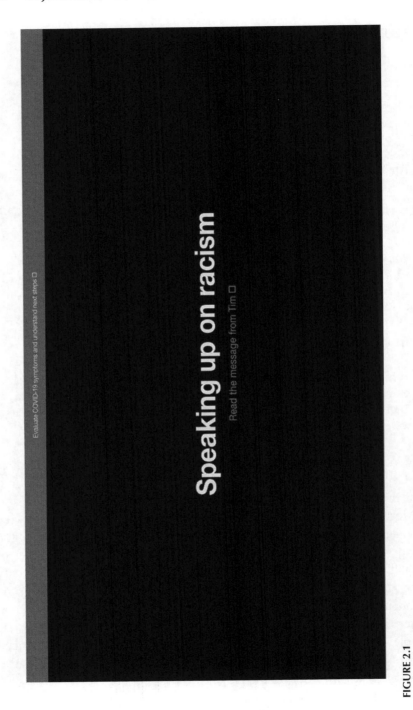

FIGURE 2.1

Apple's website homepage after the death of George Floyd

Social Justice and Equity and Office Water Coolers

Ceah Justice is a trainer in leadership and intersectionality. An uncompromising advocate for social change, Justice is a gay Black woman. She called out how employee engagement pushed corporate response. Justice explained,

> A lot of that change happened because as employees that were impacted, we stood up and said, "Listen, I've got to come to work, and you want me to come to work. That guy that just got shot in the street is the same age as my son, right? I have twin boys. They're 20, and you expect me to come to work and perform my job to the best of my ability? And you're not even recognizing the impact this has on us?"

With the George Floyd coverage everywhere across all digital channels, Justice sighed, "You can't escape. You know what's happening around you, but you're not responding to me as an employee and in an empathetic way."

She noted how employees banded together at T-Mobile, where Justice worked until 2021, to say, "You better do something about this or you're going to see this mass exodus of people. You're going to see morale tank, and in a sales environment that's the last thing you want to happen." As a result, T-Mobile was an example of an enterprise that looked at how to address racial injustice because employees demanded it. Justice shared,

> We literally got together. We called ourselves the Black delegation at the time, and we got together, and there's no list of all the Black people at a company, right? It was just we had a team. We had Teams, we had Slack, and we just started adding other people that were impacted in our circles. We had this massive meeting that I led, and it was like, "Listen, I know. I know that everybody is upset. We're sitting around complaining, but what are we going to do about it? Right. We have a voice."

Because there was an environment at T-Mobile where employees could speak up, they did.

> People felt safe to be able to say, "You know what—the way that we're operating, it's not good. I don't see this representation here and here. And it's important that we're reflecting the communities that we serve. And we're not doing that right now."

Those conversations at T-Mobile were led by the same people within communities that translated to employee activism, which led to changes being made.

Saliently, the technology company with the world's largest market valuation, Apple, contributed to corporate advocacy and support for social justice. As Michael Burns called out in our interview: "For a full week, if you went to Apple.com, there was no logo, no Apple products. The site just referred to the Black Lives Matter spirit on a black screen," Burns illuminated, adding his belief that this would not have happened pre-COVID: "We have plenty of data points that support that. George Floyd wasn't the first person who suffered death tied to police violence, but employee engagement put the pressure on corporations."

Leading with Purpose

These observations and foundational shifts in the understanding, awareness, and attitudes toward social equity have expanded to more senior executive conversations in boardrooms and C-suite water coolers. Corporations have begun to investigate their own DEI policies more seriously and how their structural institutions might have systemic limitations that included bias or did not include diverse viewpoints.

For example, Justice told us how T-Mobile investigated its franchise/third-party retailer model and found that people of color were vastly underrepresented. At T-Mobile, third-party retailers provide 60–70% of the retail business, but Justice noted, "No one had taken the time to look to see if we had proper representation." As they gathered data, T-Mobile found they didn't have any Asian owners, or African American women owners. The million-dollar franchise entry fee was a barrier to entry, and that was embarrassing for the company. Subsequently they worked with banks and incubator programs to try and address that barrier to entry. Justice demonstrated her innovation in leadership to tackle this enhanced focus: "It's not enough for us to just be working in this company," she said of herself and her Black colleagues.

> We need to be leading this company as well. Part of that is we have got to start digging back, peeling back the layers of the onion to see what is wrong—how we're responding culturally, what's happening with our policies and our procedures—all the systemic systems that are in place.

Yvonne Wolf noted,

> My big message during that time was, if you are not creating systems where all belong, you're creating systems where some belong. I got a little provocative by pointing out that Human Resources is complicit in the results we're seeing. HR has been forever blaming management. We don't have diverse talent. We don't have a pipeline.

Often, that is at least in part the result of unequal representation in important positions. "Who in the world is creating the systems and practices that they're working in? If you notice, the majority of CHROs are actually white leaders," Wolf noted. The pandemic had the effect of blurring lines between personal and professional, between community and business. In corporate boardrooms around the world, ESG mandates are more pronounced than ever, with the S, for Social, being catalyzed by community and advanced in corporate with focus on talent engagement. Without diversity in leadership as well, though, all this energy will still not make meaningful change.

Love Your Brand, Customers Love You

Beyond George Floyd and Black Lives Matter, we see community movements—and resulting consumer attitudes—driving corporate modeling, advertising, and branding tones. Sustainability is one of the arenas where this is most easily seen. Brands like Cotopaxi and Patagonia have made sustainability a central tenet of their branding. That appeals to a certain demographic, particularly among millennials and Gen Z consumers who may be more aware of climate change than older buyers, for instance.

In Patagonia's case, the narrative is well known: Yvon Chouinard founded the company in 1973 and has consistently ensured that his company has been one of the outdoor brands at the forefront of sustainability, particularly among textile brands. Seeing how corporate execs had begun to wear Patagonia products regularly, Chouinard announced in 2019 that it would limit its branded product partnership to firms passing certain ESG benchmarks.

In 2022, Chouinard took further steps, declaring that Patagonia's ownership would be transferred to the Patagonia Purpose Trust, thus ensuring profits would go to addressing climate change and protecting undeveloped land worldwide. In 2017 and 2019, respectively, Patagonia launched its Worn Wear and ReCrafted programs toward repairing and upcycling, supplementing the previously existing commitment to One Percent for the Planet, an initiative of which Chouinard was a founding member back in 1985. Consumers are paying attention. The 2021 Axios–Harris Poll 100 led consumers to name Patagonia the American company with the best reputation—largely because of its focus on philanthropy and environmentalism.[4]

Columbia Sportswear is similarly trusted. It ranked number one in brand values and trust in Forbes's inaugural Halo 100 list in 2021.[5] Even if Columbia is less visible than Patagonia about its social stances and sustainability efforts, consumers know and trust its products for their durability and innovation. Products that last are inherently more sustainable, and consumers trust and appreciate Columbia Sportswear for exactly this reason. That sustainability is simply good business, as our interviewees noted. As Bracken Darrell, President and CEO of Logitech, noted in our interview, "Humans will make companies be human. Give me the choice between a company that's carbon neutral or climate positive and one that's not, and all things created equal, it's a no-brainer."

From Z to Alpha: Generational Relations

Perceptions are changing, with consumers recognizing that every action and every choice is political. While individual consumer choices may not carry the same weight as systemic change or corporate policy in helping craft a sustainable future for our planet, every purchase we make as consumers tells brands, explicitly or implicitly, that we accept what they do to offer us their product or service at those prices.

When we talked to Marisa Goldbenburg, President of the Princeton Alumni Association in Austin, about the book project, and how we were interested in engaging voices from Generation Alpha (the generation born between 2010 and 2015), she mentioned that her then 13-year-old son Josh focused on sustainability in his Bar Mitzvah presentation. When we talked to Josh, he agreed that every choice we make as humans is political, and every choice should have global sensitivities. He told us that he thinks about island nations and their futures with climate change and rising sea levels. Climate change is coming, and it is a global issue. In-fighting and a stagnant two-party system are not the answer. Nationalism and regionalism will not solve climate change. Josh said, "I want to see a less divided political system and a more internationalized trade system and government. I'm an internationalist, and I think that international ties are a key factor for a successful government."

When we asked Josh what he thought the keys to a more sustainable and just future might be, he was incredibly thoughtful and succinct. "First of all, I support the Green New Deal," he explained, "We need to quickly divert all our actions away from fossil fuels and coal and all these things that emit toxic chemicals into the air." He pointed to the agricultural sector as a place to start, "because they contribute so much of our greenhouse gases. Regulation of agriculture companies is a first step." He added that from an economic standpoint, while moving away from fossil fuels might cost jobs, embracing clean energy opens up other jobs. This sort of pragmatic, forward-looking thought is emblematic of the younger generations.

Similarly, Jen Cohen related a story about her daughter. "My daughter did Girls Who Code, which gave her a guaranteed internship with a company, but she wouldn't take it." Cohen said her daughter told her, "I don't like their business practices. I don't want to work for them." Cohen went further, noting that,

> In talking with her college friends, that's the norm now. They don't like how people were treated, so they're not going to work there. I see younger people—even just ten years younger—with an unwillingness to accept things I had no choice but to accept. They're calling it out.

Kim Yapchai, Senior Vice President and Chief Environmental Social and Governance Officer at Tenneco, reminded us of research from the Edelman Trust Institute that shows people trust companies more than governments.[6] Agreeing that companies have become more responsive to social issues, she also noted that Gen Z is helping drive those changes. "What they're for in a company," she said, "is that it's aligned with ESG. Whether you're looking at it from diversity or sustainability or career development, they have options and can be more critical in their choices."

The Rise of B-Corps

Benefit corporations (B-corps) exemplify how community movements inform consumer choices that then influence corporate structure and purpose. B-corps are a relatively recent corporate structure option—Maryland was the first US state to formally recognize them in 2010. B-corps are a private certification of corporations administered by B Lab Global, a global nonprofit that certifies companies that meet particular sustainability thresholds. Companies must meet a minimum score from an assessment of social and environmental performance, integrate B-corps commitments to stakeholders (as opposed to shareholders) into company governance, and pay an annual fee based on annual sales. This certification must be renewed every three years. Some of the fastest-growing and most-trusted brands (at least when it comes to perceptions of sustainability) are certified B-corps: Allbirds, Ben & Jerry's, Bombas, Cotopaxi, Patagonia, Prose, Toms, and many others. In 2021 (yes, again, at the height of the pandemic), the organization that certifies B-corp status, B Lab Global, indicated that they had received more than 6,000 applications for certification from businesses—a 38% increase compared to the period from 2018 to 2019.

A recent *Forbes* article showcased a survey on B-corps conducted by Sezzle, a fintech company, that showed 81% of respondents said that it is important for them to purchase from brands that align with their social values, and 80% stated they would pay for a sustainable product. As noted by the CEO of Sezzle, Charlie Youakim, "Millennials, Gen-Z, and the generations that follow them are becoming more and more loyal to companies that not only talk about social good but act on it. They extend trust towards purpose-driven brands."[7] During the pandemic, and with the increasing purchasing power of younger generations, consumer motivations are leaning toward more social or environmental, and principled around purpose—an elevation of motivation above just pure capitalistic pursuit of profit.

Applied Altruism

Altruism is inherently human because it is emotionally rewarding. The sentiment is something that social equity movements can tap into and arguably should use to their advantage. Applied altruism is a philosophical and social movement that uses evidence and reason to determine how to benefit others as much as possible. Then they act on that basis, to further progress in "normal" times and survive a pandemic in the most extreme of times like the turn of this past decade.

Marilyn Chaplin, Chief Human Resources Officer at NTT, spoke to similar themes when she shared employee sentiment. "They really want to join a company that is deeply committed, and that has the opportunity to make a sustainable difference." That purpose—that sense of being part of something important, the sense of being part of something forward-facing—is part of building life satisfaction. Barbara Adachi compared it to the Japanese idea of "ganbaru"—working through something until it is completed, the purpose of working through perseverance.

Carolina Aguilar, CEO and Co-Founder of INBRAIN Neuroelectronics, looked at how we are evolving as intelligent beings, referencing Ken Wilber's "theory of everything" that makes sense of how all the world's knowledge systems fit together and elevate our awareness. Wilber's illumination of this belief is represented in his writings such as the book, *Integral Life Practice: A 21st-Century Blueprint for Physical Health, Emotional Balance, Mental Clarity, and Spiritual Awakening.*[8] In reflection to Wilber's writings and within the context of the pandemic, Aguilar pointed to how human civilizations and progress are grappling with narcissism, ego, and the need to be self-serving, against the broader opportunity to function as a collective whole. "Awakening means there are more differences in perspectives than we absorbed new values and we counteract all that egocentrism that makes us just look about ourselves, our lives."

The shared nightmare of the pandemic was a moment in time for us to experience, in various ways, our shared and collective experience—no matter what race, economic standing, or belief system, we were all made vulnerable to the impact of COVID-19 and had to work together as societies and communities to minimize travesties to the integrity of our health, communities, and economies. We can use these same principles in building sustainable community movements that were tangible during the pandemic. We have this remarkable opportunity to extrapolate beyond the "White Swan" moments of energy and movement toward more sustainable futures—whether by way of applied altruism or harnessing our instinct to innovate and evolve as a global community.

Unevenly Distributed Momentum

While effects of the pandemic electrified, amplified, and magnified the focus on social sustainability, the responsibility still lies with those of us driving toward lasting change. We already observed the possibility that the energy is dissipating in the post-pandemic "new normal."

Barbara Adachi spent 23 years as a Deloitte partner and currently serves on corporate boards. When we originally spoke, Adachi had just stepped down as president of the International Women's Forum (IWF) in Northern California—she spearheaded important initiatives to help transform the organization.

> One of the initiatives that I'm most proud of during my presidency— which spanned the entire time of COVID is launching a group called the Champions of Racial Equality (CoRE). CoRE defined a safe space to have conversations and provide education around racial equality for our members and remains an integral part of IWF Northern California today.

But she ran into the same problem so many community movement organizers historically have, that of maintaining momentum. "We're having our two-year anniversary and we're saying, how do we keep the conversations alive and our members engaged? We have to keep tying in other social issues into the conversation to ensure it remains relevant." We cannot let meaningful community movements run out of steam simply because there are new distractions and less focus on the common experiences catalyzed by a global pandemic. This is especially true, as we see so many of these community movements beginning to lead to meaningful policy and societal changes.

While movements around social sustainability wax and wane on the fulcrum of human emotion—intensified during the pandemic—we should be mindful of the direction in which the movements lean. In recent years, we have seen a tremendous rise in book bans and curriculum challenges of progressive mindsets, just as we've also seen a rise in demonstrations on behalf of more equal rights. The tension that sometimes arises as a result was brought up by Noha White in our conversation. Chief Information Officer at Detroit Diesel Company, White noted this tension is often rooted in an emotional response to a swiftly changing world around us. At the start of the pandemic, White said she was optimistic that, "We would actually see ourselves in the mirror better and maybe even make a change for the better," especially given this political dynamic where sometimes it feels like "we're going backward." She noted that people are the most important element of creating change but also, "people are generally scared." And fatigue and exhaustion play a role, too. "It's obvious that we need to take care of each other, and people are really the most important asset, but maybe they don't have enough energy to do anything else."

And so we find ourselves in this situation where we have a great deal of social fighting amidst an ongoing barrage of uncertainties. White pointed to the fight for rights: "It's hypocritical because they argue no mandates, right? But then, at the same time, they're attacking other people's rights, whether it's females or Blacks or voters." As she noted, "I'm not even sure what it is they're afraid of. They're afraid of something, but they're not *for* anything. It's like, what are you for instead? Let's work on those."

We see people sometimes voting against what would be best for their community because they are afraid, and because they are uncertain of a changing world. "Why are you fighting so hard against your own self-interests?" White asked. She pointed to younger generations as an example of how to fight through that. "Their focus is on the community," she said, "and the people and not necessarily the politics." In some ways, White sees all this as countering the idea of a "social consciousness rising," which was something that came up through the course of our research. Of course, both things can be true. People can be afraid of uncertainty and react out of fear, just as people can awaken to a greater social consciousness. Sometimes people can hold both of those opposing things at once in response to each other. People are complex—even as emotions are basic and theoretically simple.

Perhaps that is one of the biggest lessons we can all take from community movements. People are complex. They are motivated by a wide range of emotions and circumstances, and the pandemic dramatically advanced that range to the very forefront of the global human experience—at home and at work.

Capitalism through a Sustainability Prism

While corporations wrangled with the bottom-up community influence on social equity issues, and the impact on how they engage with communities where they operate (as well as their own talent management), the purpose of enterprise became increasingly multifaceted during the pandemic. Entering from backstage: "*stakeholder* capitalism" to displace "*shareholder* capitalism."

Traditional shareholder capitalism centers on the idea that corporations should focus on what will return the greatest profits (dividends) for shareholders. Stakeholder capitalism, by contrast, proposes corporations should serve the interests of all their stakeholders—meaning not just investors and owners, but all employees, vendors, customers, and the public at large—rather than just shareholders. Instead of maximizing profits, the emphasis is on long-term value creation and sustainable growth. If we can look to the 1980s and 1990s for the advent and rise of shareholder primacy (perfect examples: *Wall Street*, and *Wolf of Wall Street*), the last few decades have, for many corporations, helped point toward stakeholder capitalism as a healthier alternative.

In the 50th Annual Meeting of the World Economic Forum (WEF) in Davos in 2020, world leaders heralded stakeholder capitalism and the central theme "Stakeholders for a Cohesive and Sustainable World."[9] As part of that event, the WEF updated its Davos Manifesto—the guiding principles of the event—for the first time in over 40 years. The revision now states that "the purpose of a company is to engage all its stakeholders in shared and sustained value creation." Similarly, the manifesto has been revised to note that companies should have zero tolerance for corruption, pay their fair share of taxes, and uphold human rights. Davos is reflective of changing corporate culture at organizations worldwide. Funding priorities are changing, and board members—as well as corporate executives—are expecting more multithreaded examples of how impact will be driven by an organization. One of which is most readily visible is diversity in leadership roles.

Her Leadership

Cooper Hefner, son of Hugh Hefner from Playboy Enterprises, army reservist, and now a venture capitalist, touched on this in our conversation.

> I believe there are a lot of people who are younger who just sit there scratching their heads, wondering how are there not more female CEOs leading

Fortune 500 and Fortune 1000 companies? How are there not more women who are leaders in boardrooms?

In his career, he said, has had the opportunity to work with numerous women who were entrepreneurs or who were founders—and it was not until he was older and more established in his own career that he realized that was not always the case. And, he said, "When you look at the world through that lens, naturally you do have the desire to think through how to participate and encourage on the environmental, social, and corporate governance front, with ESG."

Noting how Playboy recently changed a title from Chief Human Resources Officer to Chief People Officer, Heffner continued,

> You move in a direction where you hope that the head of HR is not just protecting the company, but actually minding the culture and the people who are there. It's quite strange that the role historically had not participated in a board room. You have a moment, and you realize, "Hey, why has this not been done?" If you're in a position where you have a voice (which most of us do), or even better, you're in a position where you have the levers of power at your disposal—then you have an obligation to course correct or otherwise do what you can.

The role of leadership in the new capitalism paradigm has also shifted. The focus on multiple stakeholders necessarily means that greater diversity of background, color, race, beliefs, etc. is needed in the C-suite and in the boardroom. Meanwhile, the impact of the pandemic on the human experience has significantly magnified the focus on talent as *people*, as humans, rather than the more clinical view of *resources*.

Among the many insights offered by Bracken Darrell, the exceptional CEO of Logitech at the time of our interviews, he explained how companies might be tempted to greenwash their ESG metrics, especially as the SEC is working toward better defining those metrics. Darrell told us he thought some of these changes might be here to stay,

> Because I think it is about profits, and I'm probably in a slightly different camp than most people on this one. I don't think that the solution is a balanced scorecard—that we need to stop thinking about profits only for companies.

We need to think about being good for the world, for the planet, et cetera. I think you don't have a choice. I think that companies won't be given the alternative. Customers won't allow it. So, I don't think this is a noble act on behalf of companies or investors even to decide that profits no longer are the only way we should measure companies; humanity is forcing it. The good news is it just simply aligns corporate success and return on shareholder investment with DEI and environmental sustainability.

We come back to this idea in much more depth when we look at corporate engagement, but Darrell's point remains incredibly salient. Our shared experienced humanity is forcing these changes. Multiple stakeholders across communities are demanding greater equity, accountability, transparency, and inclusion in the value exchange of family, community, and business. The multi-stakeholder community is itself, a community.

Memes, the Block(buster)chain, and Financial Equity

Blockchain popularization and the role of memes illuminate other ways that the explosion of social media access and communication advanced community movement toward equity—in this case, financial equity. In particular, Robinhood, an online trading platform, was a key part of an investing revolution at the beginning of the pandemic, fueled by new investors who were attracted to its ease of use, low barrier to entry, and historically low stock prices with the initial market pull-back from the pandemic. For the first time, young and novice investors felt they had the power to trade and control how to invest their money. The growth was further accelerated by the remarkable disruption caused by meme-investing—when social media platforms like Reddit inspired day trading of heavily shorted stocks like GameStop in 2021, resulting in new unimagined millionaire status by your "ordinary guy or gal" when the stock rose from US$40 to US$400 within just a few days.[10]

Meanwhile, cryptocurrency exchanges similarly took off during the pandemic and, like Robinhood, there are narratives that would suggest both that it offers greater democratization of funds and greater opportunities for further expanding the digital divide and concentration of wealth. For instance, a 2022 Ariel–Schwab Black Investor Survey found that 25% of Black American respondents owned cryptocurrencies, and that number was a far higher 38% for Black investors under the age of 40.[11]

That correlated with other findings that Black respondents were generally less trusting of the stock market and traditional financial institutions than white respondents. Similarly, a recent NORC survey from the University of Chicago found that 44% of American cryptocurrency investors were people of color.[12]

Both population groups have traditionally been underserved by financial institutions. Blockchain technologies that advanced during the pandemic fueled greater inclusion in financial awareness, wealth, and intelligence. As E. David Ellington shared with us:

> I think the overwhelming majority of people still believe in the mainstream markets. But people know there's a political element to it all with a libertarian kind of perspective. The frustration of how the government "handled" COVID. Therefore, this is a rebellious kind of thing—what is this alternative currency that the government does not control? Here's something that's not controlled by the government, which I think is incompetent.

The counter-culturalism that electrified social media and pulled a variety of stakeholders into financial systems was unprecedented.

In talking to Jaslyn Wang, Director with crypto pioneer, Polygon, he shared the swift shift in dynamics during the pandemic. Polygon has been one of the changemakers in the field of cryptocurrency to light the path forward for how the industry invests in technology-powered sustainability and human capital investment. Wang noted,

> We were originally here for the technology, and then it kind of exploded, and adoption was phenomenal. We were working with traditional enterprises, and there were a lot of questions regarding sustainability. What's our strategy? What's our approach? How serious are we about this? And that's kind of how it started.

Subsequently, Polygon experienced a meteoric rise during the pandemic due to a few key factors:

- Scalability for faster and cheaper transactions.
- Seamless and cost-effective user experience for decentralized finance (DeFi) projects.
- Favorability as a choice for non-fungible tokens (NFTs).
- Developer-friendly ecosystems.

- Active partnership and integration pursuits.
- Strong community support.

With this success, Wang recognized,

> That's where we thought if we want to truly work toward mass adoption—not just for Polygon but in our community—we need to really step up. We need to realize our role in this society is a lot larger than what we were originally here for.

Granted, as the pandemic was ebbing, the world witnessed a significant "Crypto Winter." In December 2022, a *Washington Post* article noted, "Crypto Winter has come. And it is looking more like an ice age. Prices have crashed, investors are walking away, and Sam Bankman-Fried is in jail. It is not clear if the industry can recover."[13] Yet, seven months later, as we were finalizing this manuscript, Bitcoin prices had bounced back from a low of US$16,000 in December 2022, to almost double that in July 2023. Meanwhile, esteemed institutions like Fidelity Investments (Figure 2.2)[14] have started to offer Crypto ETFs. In this way the Great Digitalization delineated in Chapter 1 had the effect of addressing a facet of inequity in communities—financial access and equity—via cryptocurrencies and the blockchain.

From Moments to Movements

At a scale greater than either of the world wars, a microscopic protein created a common experience that, in turn, amplified the power of the *common* communities. COVID-19 was the ultimate humanization event of our history. The humanization fostered dynamics that influenced movement around social equity and sustainability of under-represented communities from the bottom up, to counter the top-down power politics that have historically prevailed in business. Various leaders we interviewed believe that the ethos of stakeholder capitalism is here to stay. Even if old, unsustainable, habits return, the sustainability imperative as a critical measure of corporate value is thankfully more than ever intertwined with corporate DNA.

FIGURE 2.2
Fidelity (investment brokerage service) website homepage with banner promoting crypto trading

NOTES

1. Dunivin, Z., Yan, H., Ince, J., & Rojas, F. (2022). Black Lives Matter protests shift public discourse. *The Proceedings of the National Academy of Sciences,* 119(10). https://www.pnas.org/doi/full/10.1073/pnas.2117320119
2. Cullors, P. (2020, January 1). Black lives matter began after Trayvon Martin's death. Ferguson showed its staying power. *NBC News.* https://www.nbcnews.com/think/opinion/black-lives-matter-began-after-trayvon-martin-s-death-ferguson-ncna1106651
3. @Rika Nakazawa
4. Axios. (2021, May 13). *The 2021 Axios Harris Poll 100 Reputation Rankings.* https://www.axios.com/2021/05/13/the-2021-axios-harris-poll-100-reputation-rankings
5. McGregor, J. (2021, December 16). How Columbia sportswear became America's most trusted brand. *Forbes.* https://www.forbes.com/sites/jenamcgregor/2021/12/16/how-columbia-sportswear-became-americas-most-trusted-brand/?sh=672c4d8b317e
6. Edelman. (2022, January 18). *Edelman Trust Barometer Reveals Even Greater Expectations of Business to Lead as Government Trust Continues to Spiral.* https://www.edelman.com/news-awards/2022-edelman-trust-barometer-reveals-even-greater-expectations-business-lead-government-trust
7. Kohan, S. (2021, March 28). Customers seek purpose driven companies creating a rise in b-corps. *Forbes.* https://www.forbes.com/sites/shelleykohan/2021/03/28/customers-seek-purpose-driven-companies-creating-a-rise-in-b-corps/?sh=48f17cbf6dd2
8. Reference needed here.
9. World Economic Forum. (2020, January 14). *Stakeholder Capitalism: A Manifesto for a Cohesive and Sustainable World.* https://www.weforum.org/press/2020/01/stakeholder-capitalism-a-manifesto-for-a-cohesive-and-sustainable-world/
10. Marcus, S. (2021, January 31). *GameStop: What Happened and What to Do When the Market Opens Monday.* LinkedIn. https://www.linkedin.com/pulse/gamestop-what-happened-do-when-market-opens-monday-stacy/
11. Charles Schwab. (2022). Ariel-Schwab Black Investor Survey (2022): Longstanding disparity between Black and White investors narrows, but new risks emerge. Retrieved March 30, 2023, from https://www.schwabmoneywise.com/tools-resources/ariel-schwab-survey-2022
12. NORC at the University of Chicago. 22, July 22). *More Than One in Ten Americans Surveyed Invest in Cryptocurrencies [Press Release].* https://www.norc.org/research/library/more-than-one-in-ten-americans-surveyed-invest-in-cryptocurrenci.html
13. Mark, J., & De Vynck. (2022, December 18). Crypto winter has come and it's looking more like an ice age. *The Washington Post.* https://www.washingtonpost.com/business/2022/12/18/crypto-winter-ftx-collapse-bitcoin-prices/
14. Fidelity Investment. (2023). Trade crypto [Screenshot]. https://www.fidelity.com/crypto/trading

3

Governance and Government: Private and Public Accountabilities

MOVEMENT FROM MOTIVATION

Without the appropriate depth and breadth of "G"—Governance, the intricate components of Environmental, Social, and Governance (ESG) are rendered ineffective. While customer love, engagement, and trust serve as powerful motivators for organizations to embrace sustainability values and take action, many entities also require the "stick" to drive change. In the absence of regulations, guidelines, and consequences, the market often gravitates toward the easiest route to maximize profits.

David Eun, Chief Innovation Officer at Samsung Next and a venture partner at Valo Ventures, expounded on this carrot–stick dynamic.

> When people talk about ESG, they tend to focus on the E and not as much on the S and the G. I thought a lot of businesses and senior leaders were doing it almost like a check-the-box activity where you kind of needed it, but it was more for optics, sort of in a feel-good category. ESG was more of an ethical thing, more of a corporate integrity thing, a personal morality thing.

Eun continued, "That's not bad by itself, obviously. People are beginning to connect it to business outcomes and realizing there's more data coming out, and you're seeing there's a carrot and a stick involved here."

DOI: 10.4324/9781003462347-3

The stick, Eun explained, "is now that governments and regulators are getting into it, there's going to be a price to pay if you don't get in front of it." Regulatory bodies are getting involved. With greater compliance catalysts, along with oversight, Governance has become more critical than ever. Plus, private and public partnerships that are stewards for how enterprises expand and contribute to economic growth are more important than ever.

ACRONYM-OF-STANDARDS

There is an abundance of standards and frameworks available for organizations to align with. Throughout the pandemic, an increasing number of enterprises aimed to publish reports and credentials regarding sustainability measurements, showcasing their contributions to one or more UN SDG (Sustainable Development Goals). Simultaneously, government mandates are also on the rise. For instance, the US Securities and Exchange Commission (SEC) introduced a proposed climate risk disclosure rule for publicly traded companies, necessitating the integration of climate risk assessment into their materiality evaluation and overall risk management strategies. Similarly, the European Union's Corporate Sustainability Reporting Directive came into effect in January 2023, obligating approximately 50,000 companies to disclose business risks and opportunities associated with social and environmental matters, as well as the impact of their operations on people and the planet. Initial reporting requirements are set to be implemented in 2025.

Pick a Card, Any Card

While there is no universally recognized "golden seal" for ESG reporting, several standards bodies have merged and consolidated their frameworks. The most prominent ones today are as follows:

1. IFRS Sustainability Disclosure Standards: Developed by the International Sustainability Standards Board (ISSB) under the International Financial Reporting Standards (IFRS) Foundation, these new standards aim to create a unified set of disclosure requirements for reporting ESG data globally. They encompass both

general sustainability-related financial information and specific disclosures regarding climate-related risks and opportunities.

2. Sustainability Accounting Standards Board Standards: Initially established by the Sustainability Accounting Standards Board (SASB) in 2018, the SASB Standards outline guidelines for disclosing financially material sustainability information across 77 industries. These standards identify relevant subsets of ESG issues for each industry, including specific considerations for various IT products and services. In 2021, the SASB Standards were incorporated into the Value Reporting Foundation, which was subsequently absorbed by the IFRS Foundation in 2022. The SASB Standards remain in use until the release of the new IFRS standards.

3. Climate Disclosure Standards Board Framework: Developed by the Climate Disclosure Standards Board (CDSB), this framework supports the inclusion of ESG reporting in mainstream corporate reports such as annual reports and 10-K filings. Initially released in 2010 with a focus on climate impact, the framework expanded in 2015 to incorporate broader environmental considerations. However, after the CDSB's consolidation into the IFRS Foundation in 2022, no further work is being conducted on this framework.

4. Global Reporting Initiative Standards: Developed by the Global Reporting Initiative (GRI), these standards enable organizations of all sizes, both private and public, to understand and report on their economic, environmental, and social impacts in a comparable and credible manner. The GRI Standards comprise universal, sector-specific, and topic-based sustainability reporting guidelines. They are not only relevant to reporting companies but also to investors, government policymakers, and other stakeholders.

5. Carbon Disclosure Project: Formerly known as the Carbon Disclosure Project, CDP is a nonprofit organization founded in 2000. It operates an environmental disclosure system that allows companies to report on their business risks and opportunities related to climate change, water security, and deforestation through separate questionnaires. CDP assigns letter-grade scores in each area, which can be accessed by various stakeholders. City governments can also use the CDP disclosure system to report on their climate action efforts and other environmental data.

6. Task Force on Climate-related Financial Disclosures: Established in 2015 by the Financial Stability Board, the Task Force on Climate-related Financial Disclosures (TCFD) develops recommendations for companies to disclose information on their financial risks associated with climate change. These recommendations are intended for use by investors, lenders, and insurance underwriters. The TCFD's 11 recommendations focus on governance, strategy, risk management, and climate-related metrics and targets.

7. United Nations Global Compact: Launched in 2000, the UN Global Compact is considered the world's largest corporate sustainability initiative. It emphasizes aligning business strategies and operations with ten principles encompassing human rights, labor practices, the environment, and anti-corruption measures. Participating companies submit an annual Communication on Progress (CoP) report detailing their adherence to these principles. In 2023, the Global Compact introduced a new digital platform for CoP submissions, replacing the narrative format with a standardized questionnaire. Additionally, businesses can report their contributions to and impact on the UN's Sustainable Development Goals through a separate platform that combines the Global Compact's principles with the GRI Standards.

8. Science-Based Targets initiative: The Science-Based Targets initiative (SBTi) is a partnership with CDP, the UN Global Compact, the World Resources Institute and the World Wide Fund for Nature. The targets they set show enterprises how much and how quickly they need to reduce their greenhouse gas (GHG) emissions to mitigate the worst effects of climate change. As per their website, the SBTi:

   • Defines and promotes best practice in emissions reductions and net-zero targets in line with climate science.
   • Provides technical assistance and expert resources to companies which set science-based targets in line with the latest climate science.
   • Brings together a team of experts to provide companies with independent assessment and validation of targets.
   • The SBTi was the lead partner of the Business Ambition for 1.5°C campaign—an urgent call to action from a global coalition of UN agencies, business, and industry leaders, which mobilized companies to set net-zero science-based targets in line with a 1.5°C future.

7. Workforce Disclosure Initiative. A distinctly non-climate-impact initiative, the Workforce Disclosure Initiative (WDI) was created in 2016 a charity that supports responsible investment practices with an ESG focus. The WDI framework is modeled on the CDP's disclosure system with an online survey—which asks about topics that include workplace health and safety, policies, and practices to support employee well-being, and treatment of both internal employees and supply chain workers—delivers to business a benchmark against their peers.

8. EcoVadis. A web-based assessment service that rates the sustainability practices and operations of an enterprise across four vectors: Environmental Impact, Labor and Human Rights Standards, Ethics, and Procurement Practices. EcoVadis leverages thorough analysis of documentation and is built on sustainability standards like GRI (mentioned above).

Notably, the pandemic was a Petri dish in which popularity of this standard ballooned and organizations are likely to use more than one of these standards—especially multinational enterprises that operate in different regions that might have a different set of requirements. SBTi commitments and target approval rates increased at a record pace in 2021—three times faster than in 2020—with more than 1,300 companies committed to targets, at a rate of over 110 companies per month, compared with 35 companies per month at the start of the pandemic in 2020.[1] And in 2022, EcoVadis saw a 50% growth over 12 months, and raised US$500 million to accelerate the rapid pace of adoption by organizations all over the world.[2]

RIGHT FOR THE RIGHT REASONS?

Kaoru Inoue, the Director of the Global Enabling Sustainability Initiative (GeSI) in Brussels, pointed to some of the accountability frameworks as reasons for both optimism and pessimism. She highlighted that "Some of the companies have been trying to look at the different tools within their existing operations. When you have different frameworks like CDP and SBTi, GRI—all these different frameworks and standards." Inoue prompted,

The question is what existing tools do they have, or they're currently using that could meet those? And, if they don't meet these different metrics or questions, which ones do they choose? Because more and more the market for ESG ratings and all that is only growing.

Inoue noted, however, that "My perspective is still that it's all quite shallow. It's used in CSR reports. It's used in annual reports. But when you really dig into this, there's not much evidence there. It all goes back to how companies are operationalizing things." "So," she continued, "We'll get applications from very big companies saying, 'Oh, this looks great. It's a Commission project. We have also been looking into ESG and green tech. We want to join'." But, Inoue added,

> Once we start questioning them about their climate commitments, they will more often than not just link me to a blog post that says we're Year 2030-aligned, 2040-, 2050-aligned. When you go deeper into the science, and you question them on validation—again going to the specific tools that they use to validate—there's not much evidence there.

She noted that so far, the coalition has only accepted about a third of the applications as a result.

Meanwhile, Inoue noted that all too often, companies are not held to account. Right now, she said, there are very few consequences for failures to meet the standards set. Companies might say that a report is in process, or they will claim to be reporting on CDP, but there will be no public evidence even as it's still on their website. "No one's really, in my opinion, challenging them," Inoue said. And even when those companies are challenged, she explained, "The worst that will happen is they'll get kicked out, or they won't be named in certain reports. There's no active calling-out."

Inoue pointed to her time at Oxfam, a coalition of non-profits focused on alleviating poverty around the world,[3] as an example of what could work. "We had this campaign called 'Behind the Brands,' that explored the food system and the specific brands that claim to be all about fair trade, no child labor—those types of metrics." Oxfam would grade each brand from A to F, Inoue said. "When there was evidence of child labor, for example, they put out a press release. They put out tons of reports. They reported it. They sent the report to the BBC, CNN, and to all these different media companies." She said the consequences were manifested in public shame, which, of course then resulted in tremendous public relations issues for the companies cited. "So," Inoue said, "I think if it's not a big splash, a lot of companies are not really going to respond."

MEASUREMENT ... OK, BUT WHERE'S THE ACTION?

Once organizations can baseline themselves to standards, the next step must be authentic transformation. As Luis Neves insisted "Where many companies now are looking to those traditional indicators are CDPs, GRI, they are of measurement. There has been adaptation of measurement tools. But there has not been yet transformation. We need fundamental transformation to shift those measurements in the right direction. We need to use ESG as a fundamental business driver of the transformation." Neves continued, "It is not only about reporting. Do you have a target here. Do you have a standard? There are many more requirements. Businesses fulfill those minimal requirements, but those minimum requirements are there, like ISO 9000 certification."

In this way, ESG standards are becoming a minimum threshold, Neves said. "Businesses need to do this because it's part of the mainstream; the climate discussion is very present. Governments are regulating. The European Union (EU) is putting a lot of pressure on products and on standards of taxonomy." Sure enough, the EU continues to advance its regulatory environment with respect to climate action. In 2021, in the middle of the pandemic, the EU passed the European Climate Law, as part of the European Green Deal. This law includes climate neutrality, greenhouse gas emission targets, climate action plan, guidance for adaption and resilience, and, per the point of this chapter: governance and accountability. The intensification of the sustainability agenda remains unevenly distributed. The hope is that global interconnectedness will create consistency of best practices—motivated by good governance and enabled by digital innovation.

As we discussed in the Technology chapter, organizations now can be equipped for better access to data, and frameworks exist to guide their sustainability efforts. However, it is crucial to consider more compelling incentives that can effectively drive behavior toward achieving our collective goals. Additionally, since challenges such as biodiversity loss, climate change, and energy consumption result from the collective actions of all, progress will be limited if only a minority takes action. This situation resembles a modern-day "prisoner's dilemma," where the choice is between collective participation in the sustainability agenda or sabotaging the progress of others for individual gain.

In our discussion within the Technology chapter, we highlighted how organizations now have the tools to access data more effectively and are guided by frameworks to pursue sustainability initiatives. Nonetheless, it is of utmost importance to consider more compelling incentives that can genuinely drive behavior toward achieving our shared goals.

This dilemma underscores the critical need for everyone to join global community endeavors to mitigate the impact of the pandemic and work together toward a sustainable future.

Performance and Compliance Are Not Binary

Kim Yapchai, the Chief ESG Officer at Tenneco we met earlier, has a unique perspective on the carrot–stick dynamic, in part because of how she paved a path to the ESG compliance arena. "I got into compliance involuntarily," she said. "It was not something that I picked, but during the 2008 recession, our legal department got downsized, so they were redistributing the work at the time. I didn't want compliance—it wasn't considered sexy or interesting. I told my General Counsel, no, I don't want that part." But Yapchai did not really have an option. "And then I thought, I need to be thankful I have a job right now," she said, "So I took it."

Yapchai found that she was good at it, though, and really enjoyed it, and in time that led to her current position as chief compliance officer. To her mind, it is a matter of doing the right AND smart thing. "To be honest with you," she said, "I don't hurt my brain too much by trying to figure out what's E, what's S, and what's G." Instead, she asks, "What's the right thing to do, what's going to make our company perform better and be stronger?"

Yapchai noted how Ethisphere each year charts the performance of the world's most ethical company designation winners against the large-cap index[4]—the award winners outperform by 25% on average. Yapchai explained, "Why is that? It's because you're not damaging your brand. You're not wasting money on fines and damages and settlements. You're operating the right way. And that's attracting the right challenge as well. You have the right culture." To Yapchai's mind, and in general in the minds of others we interviewed, compliance and performance go hand in hand. The pandemic was a tremendous disruptor to almost every aspect of business. And as with any disruption, regulatory entities were and are quick to intervene—with the purpose and intent that organizations or entities can leverage standards to bolster the industry and communities at large.

Generational Change

Organizations are experiencing a transition in their incentives, moving from a focus on simply "doing good" to "doing smart" from a compliance mapping perspective, and ideally, to "doing what will achieve high performance." As Eun highlighted in our interview, currently, the connection between feeling good about oneself and the company in the "do good" phase is somewhat reliant on perceiving certain business outcomes as positive. In the "do smart" phase, the risks associated with sustainability emphasize that doing good is indeed doing smart by mitigating risks in business operations. However, the third phase—achieving high performance—is still in the process of taking shape. This phase involves full integration, where sustainability becomes ingrained as a fundamental part of doing business. However, we have not reached that stage yet.

For the most part, we might not get there until we have a generation of leaders who have grown up in the second chapter of good being equivalent to smart. We need the leaders of tomorrow to help industries take the next step forward, that will then drive the economies of the future.

Several interviewees emphasized that businesses and organizations that want to get a head start must harness governance hygiene sooner rather than later. Businesses that prioritize ESG will be more agile in responding to the shift in what good looks like in models of governance in an increasingly globalized world order. Plus, this world order is one of increasingly integrated private and public partnerships that starts to merge corporate governance with risk and compliance factors meted out by regional governments.

GOVERNANCE IN AN INTERCONNECTED WORLD

The COVID-19 pandemic highlighted the crucial connection between local governance and global stewardship, as it revealed the profound interdependence of societal and business communities. Prior to the pandemic, supply chains were seldom a topic of concern or consideration for many of us. However, within the first few weeks of quarantine, we gained a newfound understanding of how easily major industries could be disrupted. The scarcity of essential items, such as bathroom supplies, created immediate bottlenecks in March 2020, leading to store-imposed purchase restrictions. As a result, more people now possess at least a basic understanding of supply chains within their respective industries and potentially beyond. Certain sectors experienced more pronounced impacts, with constraints in consumer sectors felt particularly acutely. Industries ranging from automobiles to construction to publishing were all confronted with supply chain challenges, compelling them to devise strategies to address immediate concerns and future-proof themselves.

Supply Chain and Sustainability—the Shared "Resilience" Denominator

The disruptions in the supply chain during the pandemic exposed the significant challenges associated with the lack of visibility and observability in commerce and trade systems. However, organizations that possessed the capability to leverage technologies and systems for data quantification, capture, analysis, and action within their supply chain demonstrated greater resilience in addressing critical issues. They were more adept at navigating the "not business as usual" paradigm that impacted the entire life cycle of product and service sourcing, development, and delivery. This principle also holds true for managing sustainability impact and having the hygiene to persist.

The Scope 1, Scope 2, and Scope 3 emissions framework (refer to Figure 3.1) is a widely adopted framework for managing sustainability goals, particularly concerning climate change dependencies. It incorporates the entire supply chain lifecycle.

By having improved visibility into their supply chains and the ability to exert control and influence over them, organizations can effectively determine how and where to prioritize their efforts in achieving sustainability goals across similar domains.

Praveen Shankar, from our earlier chapters, noted that it is not surprising that as a result of the pandemic, "Suddenly I started getting a lot of calls from the clients around green supply chain, sustainability and all those

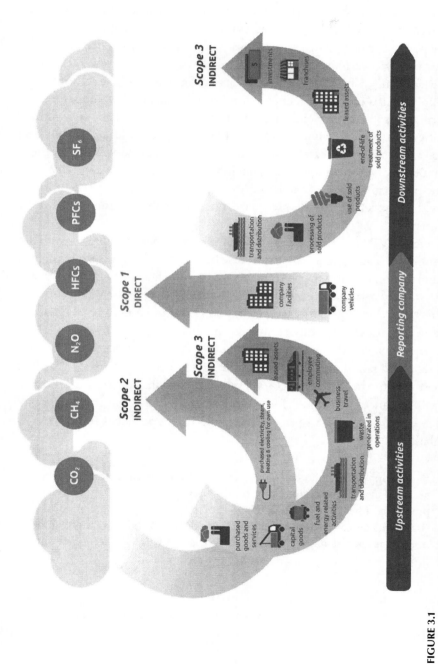

FIGURE 3.1
Illustration showing sources of Greenhouse Gas (GHG) emissions across categories defined in "Scope 1," "Scope 2," and "Scope 3"

kind of things." Rachel Payne, Portfolio Director for Climate Moonshots at Google X, said fighting climate change is "about the corporate supply chains because that's what's ultimately going to influence 90% of the emissions levels," so calls to hold corporations accountable, especially as the pandemic demonstrated the frailty of most supply chains, need to be part of any governance solutions.

Meanwhile, Christine Tiballi, CEO, and founder of DirtSat, noted that supply chains could be an entry point to governance. DirtSat focuses "on trying to solve urban challenges in terms of food security and climate mitigation. combining a lot from architecture and building science, and also from space and satellites and to see how we can solve some of those challenges." As she noted, the pandemic highlighted the need to dive into the sustainability space, particularly in how it amplified a focus in industry on the impact of the supply chain on sustainability, and particularly climate change.

The COVID-19 lockdowns resulted in a significant reduction in CO_2 emissions, leading to a visible decrease in pollution that was impossible to ignore. Many of us experienced this firsthand when we ventured outside for walks to maintain physical activity and preserve our mental well-being. This reduction in pollution served as a stark reminder of the impact of our daily activities on the environment. The disruptions in the supply chain further exposed the vulnerability and global interconnectedness of our systems. Tiballi highlighted the distressing images of farmers discarding food due to the inability to transport it from one location to another. Such instances prompted individuals to reevaluate the importance of local food systems and prioritize supporting hyper-local initiatives. As Tiballi put it,

> I'm dealing with urban challenges and specifically food security in urban areas. They're completely reliant on the food system, trucking, and shipping from other parts of the country—and even other parts of the world—which was detrimental to inner cities specifically. It really highlighted the need to develop stronger hyper-local models that we could use to not only provide food security but also change the way we farm.

Tiballi emphasized that transitioning to a more localized supply chain not only brings efficiency advantages but also reduces reliance on fossil fuels, lowers transportation and shipping costs, minimizes the need for refrigeration and packaging, and more. She highlighted the need for climate and food security to coexist, as the pandemic exposed vulnerabilities in both the food supply and the overall supply chain.

Furthermore, the pandemic served as a catalyst for communities to recognize the human toll associated with our supply chain. The outbreak of COVID-19 in meatpacking plants, for example, prompted many consumers to reflect on the true cost of our existing agriculture and livestock supply chains, as well as the impact these systems have on the individuals working behind the scenes to ensure their smooth functioning. Moreover, the repercussions of the pandemic have shed light on the extensive distances that our goods traverse. Instances of proposed railroad strikes and discussions of potential long-distance trucker strikes have revealed the inherent fragility of essential components within our supply chain infrastructure.

The interconnectedness of global economies and trade has brought about significant benefits, but it also means that events occurring in one part of the world can have far-reaching consequences globally. Prior to the Russian invasion of Ukraine, few Americans were aware of this interdependence, but Ukraine's status as a major global supplier of wheat and a significant source of oil for Europe became evident. The impacts of the invasion reverberated throughout these markets, leading to significant disruptions in the supply chain, ultimately affecting consumers. While the Russian invasion of Ukraine was not directly related to the pandemic, it can be presumed that the disruptions caused by COVID-19 were exacerbated by this additional factor, amplifying the severity of challenges in the global economy and supply chain, particularly in the areas of grains and energy.

The global response to the Russian invasion has largely involved attempts to impose embargoes on Russian products, showcasing a contemporary illustration of global governance aimed at influencing the actions of a single country. However, the effectiveness of these measures has been limited, partially due to the lack of universality in their implementation. Russian oligarchs have consistently found loopholes and workarounds to bypass embargoes and tariffs. This serves as a valuable perspective for understanding how actions related to ESG and climate sustainability can achieve effectiveness. In a world characterized by extensive global interconnections, governance mechanisms must possess a certain level of universality to be truly impactful.

PENDULUM SWINGS

Kevin Grayling, the Vice President and Chief Information Officer at Florida Crystals, discussed the complex impact of the pandemic on the sustainability landscape. On one hand, the pandemic amplified the focus on sustainability and drove intensified efforts toward social sustainability and addressing climate change. However, there were instances where the pandemic had an adverse effect. Grayling specifically highlighted the issue of packaging as a counterpoint to the progress made during the pandemic. While significant strides were made in sustainability measures in 2020 and 2021, there was a simultaneous increase in waste and plastic usage. Plastic gloves, test kits, takeout containers, and shipping boxes proliferated, contributing to a setback in waste and plastic management. Grayling suggested that the short-term waste generated in the past few years may surpass the waste generated in a typical five-year or even ten-year period. "If I'm honest about it," he said, "We all gave ourselves a bit of a pass, that there was a bigger problem to solve and therefore the byproduct of how we solved that when it relates to sustainability was 'affordable'."

Grayling emphasized that as demand and spending decline, we are returning to more typical levels of waste production. This trend can be attributed to a combination of inflation and reduced consumer expenditure. It follows a natural correlation wherein decreased consumption leads to a corresponding decrease in waste generation associated with consumption. Grayling further points out that, for many individuals, there is a simple trade-off: if there is an option that allows for easier actions but results in more waste, human nature tends to gravitate toward the easier choice, even if it comes at the expense of a larger ecological footprint. This observation underscores the importance of universal governance in achieving effectiveness, as it provides a framework that encourages responsible choices beyond individual preferences.

Context and Framing to Drive Sustainability Sentiment

Denise Gershbein, a global strategic innovation consultant with years as a product and service design executive, is known for framing problem spaces and creating thoughtful solutions in complex environments—a talent she was able to exercise in spades during the pandemic, especially regarding sustainability agendas across industries. She reflected on how businesses and even the military are staying ahead of the curve. "People and customers in supply chain were looking at failures and predictions on when supplies will arrive or be available and is that caused by human error or it caused by climate, etc.?" she mused. "So I have seen an uptick in the business sector and the acceptance of the reality of the issues of sustainability with climate. In some ways, society is almost behind what businesses are thinking and doing." Along with the machine of business, the military machine also must stay ahead of the curve of society, to pre-empt other potential disruptions around the world. Gerschbein noted,

> The military today operates with the knowledge that climate is causing mass disruption around the globe. And it's not just climate change. That leads to problems in healthcare, which leads to migration problems, which leads to further warfare. So some of these big institutions have already not only accepted this, but they're working towards mitigating or operating within those new scenarios that society hasn't quite caught up with yet.

In the realm of compliance, established power brokers strive to maintain an edge, adopting a predictive maintenance approach concerning stable communities and societies. They recognize that unstable communities and societies possess the potential to disrupt institutions and establishments, jeopardizing the position of current leaders. Compliance and governance for sustainability serve as a dual-purpose strategy. On one hand, they enable the preservation of control and power, while on the other hand, they ensure the long-term viability of the existing socio-political and economic equilibrium.

Governance as an Immune Response

Sometimes, the need to address disruptions or risk may not be addressed in a timely fashion. Some of the insights shared by Gill Pratt, Toyota Research Institute CEO and Chief Scientist at Toyota Motors, examined how behavioral science might inform sustainability ambitions. Pratt noted, "There is this human tendency to allow small things to go wrong for a long, long time. And then suddenly we realize that it's way too much." Then when there is a leadership and governance response, it is hard to determine if it was too dramatic or too much over-indexing for the sake of risk-management and safety. He mused that a major traumatic event, like the Gulf War, 9/11, or the COVID pandemic triggered something akin to an inflammatory response to an infection.

> The question we were trying to look at is, was the cure worse than the disease? Did the immune response to September 11 create more problems than it solved? And the answer, in the end, was that we weren't sure. There were arguments on both sides of this.

As Pratt illuminated, human psychology and sociology shape our response to various trauma and experiences. "We didn't understand how much human psychology and sociology would matter—the incredible dysfunction that occurred."

We all experienced disruptions in the supply chain, although the specific impacts may have varied. However, these shared experiences have provided us with an opportunity to diversify supply chains and become more aware of social dysfunctions. Despite the challenges posed by echo chambers and divisive politics, the problems we face are universal. To strike a balance between reactive responses and proactive risk management, stringent governance is crucial. By effectively managing governance practices, we can navigate these challenges and work toward sustainable solutions.

Investor-Driven Governance

The catalysts for governance can take many forms. Sometimes the carrot or stick can come from global strategic neighbors. Naomi Koshi brought this up in the context of changes to Japan's governance code, which, as per the thesis of this book, emerged during the pandemic. In June 2021, Japan made revisions to its Corporate Governance Code to incorporate new measures related to climate risk disclosures, gender diversity, and independent directors on boards. These revisions align with the principles of ESG. Regarding climate disclosures, the code emphasizes the need to enhance the quality and quantity of climate-related disclosures based on the recommendations of the Task Force on Climate-related Disclosure (TCFD). On the topic of diversity, Japanese companies will be encouraged to disclose policies and measurable targets aimed at promoting diversity through the appointment of women, mid-career professionals, and non-Japanese professionals. Additionally, the revised code provides guidelines for increasing the number of independent directors on boards, from at least two to at least one-third of the board, for companies listed in the Prime market segment of the Topix (Tokyo Stock Price Index).

Koshi, the former mayor of Otsu, Japan, is a former New York City-based lawyer who returned to Japan to fight for better maternity rights. In Otsu, she helped create 55 nurseries in a city of 340,000. As a result, the number of working mothers with children under five increased by 70%. Additionally, younger couples began moving to Otsu because this social service was available, reversing the population decline in the city. As a result, she has a perfect vantage of the ways in which Japanese culture and governance have changed in response, both to the pandemic and to outside pressures. As Koshi noted, "ESG is a big topic for lawyers, and to Japanese companies. Investors ask us—especially Japanese companies—to promote ESG."

Koshi brought up the number of female directors as an example. Foreign investors ask Japanese companies to have more female directors, she said, "This is a huge pressure. So the Japanese government first introduced a corporate governance board, and now it's amended and changing the number of female directors." While that number is still only at 7.5%, that's a marked increase from ten years ago—when it was just 1%. The main reason, Koshi confirms, is foreign investors.

Japan, the world's fifth-biggest carbon emitter, raised a climate goal in April 2021, pledging to trim emissions by 46% from 2013 levels by 2030 instead of its previous target of 26%. To achieve this, continued stakeholder pressure and governance play a role. As Koshi noted, "Some Japanese companies now promote that they have zero emissions, but that's mostly because of foreign investors." That reflects the universality of the need for greater focus on ESG, especially as in the aftermath of the pandemic, greater awareness of inequalities may have refocused attention on the issues.

From Anti-Fragility to Agility

Nassim Taleb, who wrote the book *Black Swan*,[5] to which this book owes its genesis, also wrote *Antifragile*,[6] in which he describes a property of systems that increase in capability to thrive as a result of stressors, shocks, volatility, noise, mistakes, faults, attacks, or failures. More specifically, antifragile is fundamentally different from the concept of resilience, which is understood as the ability to recover from failure. Antifragility is a much more powerful quality than resilience, and in many ways, is a hallmark of how we as a species can emerge from the aftermath of the pandemic. The pandemic has been the lightning rod to create this alloy toward a new era of strength as a global community. Kim Yapchai commented,

> Obviously, none of us predicted COVID would happen. Who knows what the next five years may hold for us? Is there some other new surprise that none of us could predict? Companies have learned how to adapt and be agile during this COVID base and will continue to do that going forward.

Of course, one other key ingredient to this acceleration around sustainable change is innovation, accelerated by the Great Digitalization during the pandemic. Yapchai continued,

> While all of this change can be scary and frightening. I like to look at it as just incredible opportunity in terms of innovation, of our careers, and the future for our children. I hope people can focus on the positive that all this turmoil has created.

GOVERNANCE LEVERS

Jim Adler, Managing Director and board member of Toyota Ventures and an executive advisor at Toyota Research Institute (TRI) shared his insights about the financial incentives of compliance, particularly in incentivizing things like carbon removal.

> We realized that you need to have verifiable carbon removal projects that remove carbon for a sustained period of time, and you need a clearing price for carbon. If you're going to have car removal projects that have strong enough verification that Toyota would ever want to buy any of those credits, you're going to need some kind of marketplace that makes sure that there's transparency and verifiability and some level of regulation and standardization that would give these larger players a real incentive to buy carbon removal.

As a result, Toyota Ventures chose to invest in Nori, which offers a carbon-removal cryptocurrency. In a way, investment can be a lever for governance—something we look at more closely in our chapter on the investment community.

BACKLASH AND GREENWASHING

As the saying goes, "With every action, there is an opposite and equal reaction." The surge of energy surrounding the concepts of ESG and sustainability has been met with pushback. Mark Deuitch from The Jaci Group highlighted this tension, particularly in how corporations and individuals perceive ESG. He expressed concern about the centralization of ESG, noting that it was not long ago when there was significant momentum toward it. Now, ESG has become somewhat of an anthem for certain individuals, which Deuitch anticipated would elicit resistance and pushback. "This was catalyzed by the Tesla Elon Musk issue of getting knocked out of the S&P 500 ESG index when Exxon is still there," he said.

> There have been grumblings for a while. My bigger goal would be I don't want to see SG discarded, but in its current state, it's not going to work. It might work in Europe, but it's not going to work in America, and it's not going to work for the 90% of businesses that are SMEs.

He concluded,

> So, if you want to create an impact, whether it be environmental or social or governance, can you really do that when you're excluding 90% of the businesses on the planet? So what we want to do is something akin to network effects, to propagate ESG or whatever you want to call it. It's becoming stigmatized. But what you don't want to see is it go away. You don't want to see the impetus for better governance and better environmental practices go away because the regulators and the standard setters overreached and went too far too fast, and now it's all colliding and causing problems. That's kind of where we are now.

Bill Weihl of Climate Voice (and former sustainability "czar" of Google and Facebook) spoke briefly about this tension around ESG saturation and some of the skepticism emerging from ESG-fatigue. "A lot of young people are skeptical of corporate pronouncements around ESG, purpose, etc.," he said. "A lot of it is marketing gloss, with some real stuff underneath it—while the core business, in many cases, continues to contribute to massive societal problems." In other words, while brands jumped on the bandwagon of ESG championing, in many cases they lacked the substance behind the veneer. Weihl continued, "I think ESG is in for a reckoning in the next few years. I struggle with that a lot. I think a lot of people feel real urgency on these issues: inequality, climate, access to health care, access to clean water, etc."

Weihl shed light on the darker aspects of governance, pointing out that rules, regulations, and policies are often influenced by those in positions of power and wealth. He highlighted that despite their influence, these individuals often feel a lack of personal agency. Studies conducted in the United States have shown that laws passed tend to reflect the perspectives of the wealthy rather than the average voter. Over the past 60 years, a significant portion of our culture and mindset has been shaped by affluent individuals with libertarian inclinations, resulting in a society that primarily benefits them rather than the majority. It is crucial to empower people and provide them with a genuine sense of agency. Weihl concluded, "Giving people a sense of real agency is critical, and those kinds of 'micro-moments' matter, but it's vital that people do not stop there. We need collective action to address things like climate."

We also need collective alignment on what is defined as "sustainable." Without regulation, investment funds can call themselves whatever they see fit, a point that Rachel Payne, Portfolio Director of Climate Moonshots at X (sibling company to Google at Alphabet) drove home especially clearly. "I've heard of energy funds calling themselves ESG when their portfolio is focused on oil and gas," she told me. "It's unbelievable. There's a lot of greenwashing. "Just like any opportunity in the market," Payne said,

> you're going to have opportunists who are basically charlatans, who are going out there raising capital, claiming to be one thing because it's hot. It's a hot area, and they have an arbitrage opportunity. Until regulations catch up, until standards are more widespread and well understood, until a mea-surement is more consistently applied—they're getting away with it because there's a window of time where they can arbitrage.

If governance is interpreted as convenient to a few, or applied by the few in power, then nothing can happen.

During the pandemic, "greenwashing" became increasingly prevalent in the business and media realms. However, alongside this trend, there was a notable backlash against social sustainability, particularly in the context of board diversity. Sue Lawton, Chair of World Business Women, commented on this dynamic, expressing a cynical viewpoint. According to Lawton, many large corporations engage in ESG practices because they are compelled to do so. They feel the need to appear as if they are taking the right actions. Lawton suggests that these corporations prioritize pushing the gender agenda not because of a genuine commitment to gender equality, but because it is necessary for them to secure government contracts. As Lawton explained,

> Let's look at corporations who are doing things for women entrepreneurs in the supply chain, let me use that as an example and then attach it to my cynical view. Many large corporations will say, "I support women entrepreneurs." I would very strongly question the number of contracts they have really offered.

All too often, Lawton said,

> What these businesses have done is paid a membership fee so they can write in their report, "We support women entrepreneurs," but there's no data to show that that's the case. So I'm a bit cynical about corporations doing things because it's the right thing to do.

She continued, "So put that across to the green agenda. I do think many of them are doing it because it's what you must do today to stay in the game," she added. Nonetheless, regardless of business reasons for embracing ESG measures, the fact remains that they are mostly, as Lawton put it, "actually walking the talk." There are reasons to be optimistic, as Lawton pointed out, particularly in cases where corporations possess a financial influence comparable to that of a small or even large country. When such corporations take the lead in ESG initiatives, especially in governance, it strengthens our position. The advantage lies in the continuity that corporations can offer, as opposed to governments, which often undergo frequent changes. Therefore, when corporations with significant financial power prioritize ESG practices, it can lead to more consistent and impactful outcomes. Ultimately, given the global nature of sustainability (the interconnected nature of almost everything), accountability has to fall on both private and public parties, and also motivate the collaborate between both.

Passive vs Active Governance

Tracy Barba touched on several of these points, including how Europe and the pandemic are helping drive governance. Barba is the Executive Director and Head of ESG at 500 Startups, so she brought a bit more of an investment perspective—which I think is important to consider, especially as the investment community is the next lens we want to use looking at post-pandemic sustainability and role of digital innovation.

When asked if the pandemic helped spur some of these corporate changes and greater governance, her answer was immediate. "The pandemic probably pushed it forward a bit more," she said.

> There are several drivers that are pushing a lot of this forward, and I think it requires that, right? So there's a little bit of regulation that's happening and differences in regulation in different markets. Europe has been leading in that regard, but now you're seeing more focus from SEC on things like carbon disclosure. There was definitely some of that that got spurred on with the pandemic.

As Barba noted, though, we need to be careful not to just move on and past the pandemic. She added, "I think with the pandemic, we should look back and say what lessons could be learned? That would be a smart thing, right? Versus going on to the next big thing and trying to solve for that."

Disclosure alone is too passive. There must be active engagement and creative pursuit of innovation. Barba continued.

> We were having talks with various large corporations who are focused on ethics and tech, there was a question as to access to vaccines, for example, what kind of tracking mechanisms were in place, what kinds of tools were being used to provide information and communication, and how was that in any way biased? There were a lot more discussions that I heard around that, and the role that technology and data and AI play in some conversations or considerations around how to make that better.

Without digital innovation, organizations would not even be able to scalably capture all the necessary data points, let alone leverage those data points to yield AI conclusions to further advance a sustainability strategy.

Not all innovation is inherently good or beneficial. While technological advancements have enabled organizations to improve their measurement capabilities, analyze data, and utilize AI for better decision-making, it is crucial to consider the impact on the unrepresented, particularly in terms of social sustainability. Barba emphasized the need for discussions on the ethical risks and unintended consequences associated with technology, which are gaining momentum. It is essential to integrate these considerations early in the development and funding processes of companies. The pandemic has played a role in highlighting the disparities in distribution and access, shedding light on who has access to technology and why. It has also revealed the potential for technology to address these disparities and bridge the gaps in society.

All of this is interconnected. All of this is global. All of this requires governance, but not just in an isolated way. Meaningful and scalable sustainable transformation requires multi-stakeholder engagement (both private and public) along with a mindset that embraces anti-fragility, agility, and authenticity.

Mind the Gap—NGOs Can, and Do

Sometimes, governance handed down by nation states and regions is not easily digested by organizations. The ability to bridge gaps and build corporate community safe spaces was something Jackie Steele wanted us to consider when we spoke. President and Representative Director of For Empowering Women (FEW) Japan, Steele is also CEO of enjoi Japan K.K., where she brings Diversity, Equity, and Inclusion (DEI) business strategy to corporate leaders through experiential workshops and consulting designed to shift mindset and initiate evidence-based action.

Organizations like FEW Japan and enjoi Japan K.K. not only help fill a need that needs filling, but also supplement governance in helping create a more sustainable future. As Steele explained, FEW Japan, founded in 1981, is "the only intersectional feminist-inspired, queer-positive, trans-women inclusive and multicultural umbrella women's nonprofit in Japan serving all nationalities of women to build safe space and personal/professional development."

Nonprofits and NGOs like FEW Japan can bridge the gap between corporate engagement and global governance in a way that not only supports community movements but helps create more equity and equality. That's a piece that sometimes is forgotten or overlooked but is no less important. The efforts toward inclusivity also helped drastically increase FEW Japan's reach during the pandemic. "Prior to the pandemic," Steele said,

> we were Tokyo-centric and all in-person for 39 years. We went down to 45 members in Tokyo when COVID hit. In three years, we are up to more than 275 paying individual members and eight corporate members, who are investing in our mission of women's empowerment. We have members living across Tokyo and other regions of Japan, sharing our political capital together, learning, and growing in record community-building impact.

Steele noted, "It's really not just getting women into corporate board leadership that matters in a democracy." The same is true for political positions. There are gaps between corporate power and government regulation that nonprofits and NGOs help fill; FEW Japan is a great example of an organization filling a need that is otherwise not being met.

While the sustainability imperative has gained significant attention during the pandemic, it is often government bodies and corporate entities that dominate the headlines. However, it is crucial to recognize the essential role played by NGOs, working diligently behind the scenes, in developing corporate community safe spaces that promote equity and sustainability. NGOs offer a valuable opportunity to leverage the momentum created by the pandemic and propel it toward sustainable development. By actively engaging with NGOs and establishing shared modus operandi, we can foster meaningful collaborations that drive positive change and advance our sustainability goals.

TWO BIRDS OF A SUSTAINABILITY FEATHER

Governments and governance represent distinct manifestations of the root word "govern," which refers to the management of policies, actions, and affairs, as defined by the Oxford dictionary. In the context of sustainability, these two concepts converge through the implementation of federal, state, and city policies. Such policies can create mandates through laws or regulations or provide opportunities through funding mechanisms for industries and enterprises. The pandemic exemplified how public entities expanded collaboration with private enterprises to address both a global health crisis and an economic crisis. These collaborative efforts extended to tackling the next existential crisis—sustainability—which is more long-term and catastrophic in nature. National governments worldwide took action to contain the pandemic and care for their citizens while simultaneously funding programs that supported sustainability initiatives. These initiatives encompassed various sectors such as transportation, logistics, healthcare, energy, and more, all interconnected with corporate governance and economic prudence.

In 2020, the EU embarked on a strategic undertaking known as The European Green Deal, which consists of a series of policy initiatives established by the European Commission. The primary objective of this comprehensive plan is to ensure that the EU becomes climate neutral by the year 2050. To achieve this ambitious goal, the EU intends to conduct a thorough review of existing legislation, assessing its effectiveness in addressing climate concerns. Additionally, the EU plans to introduce new legislation in key areas such as the circular economy, building renovation, biodiversity conservation, farming practices, and innovation. By addressing these critical aspects, the European Green Deal seeks to pave the way for a sustainable and climate-resilient future for the EU.[2]

Across the Atlantic, in 2022, the Biden administration achieved a significant milestone by passing the Inflation Reduction Act, which stands as the most substantial climate legislation in the history of the United States. This groundbreaking legislation sets forth ambitious goals, including a targeted reduction of US emissions by 40% by 2030 and the establishment of a net-zero economy by 2050. With an unprecedented level of funding for climate impact amounting to nearly US$370 billion, coupled with comprehensive programs designed to incentivize industry, businesses, and communities, this legislation serves as a crucial foundation for driving climate action in the world's leading global economic superpower. Its impact is expected to reverberate not only within the United States but also resonate across the rest of the world, playing a pivotal role in catalyzing the transition toward a clean energy-driven economic ecosystem.

FROM THE PODIUM OF TWO MAJOR GLOBAL CITIES

Amidst our research, we had the opportunity to delve into the role of government and governance for sustainability at a hyper-local level with two remarkable women leaders from different parts of the world. Yuriko Koike, the Governor of Tokyo, and Kate Gallego, the Mayor of Phoenix, the fifth largest city in the United States by population, shared their insights and experiences on this crucial topic.

Governor Koike made history as the first female governor to lead the world's largest city, Tokyo, measured by urban and metropolitan area. She was re-elected in 2020 amidst the onset of the pandemic. In her second term, Governor Koike announced an ambitious goal for Tokyo to reduce GHG emissions by 50% from the levels of the year 2000 by 2030. Simultaneously, she emphasized the importance of a sustainable recovery from the pandemic and launched numerous projects aimed at addressing the climate crisis while also focusing on economic and societal recovery.

During our interview, Governor Koike highlighted the interconnectedness of cities globally and stressed the need for collaboration among cities as communities. She expressed her vision for a society that not only recovers from the challenges posed by the pandemic but also becomes more resilient in the face of future crises. Recognizing that addressing crises such as infectious diseases, terrorism, and natural disasters requires collective efforts beyond the scope of individual cities or countries, Tokyo hosted a Leader's Summit in February, inviting leaders from cities around the world to foster collaboration.

Governor Koike introduced the term "SusHi-Tech" to encapsulate Tokyo's commitment to sustainable hi-tech solutions, emphasizing the pivotal role of technology in shaping the future of sustainable cities. "Sustainable technology" remains a key focus, reflecting Governor Koike's belief in harnessing innovative and sustainable technologies to drive Tokyo's sustainability agenda forward.

Phoenix Mayor Gallego ran a successful mayoral campaign in 2021, centered around a platform that prioritized "pro-sustainability," equity, and job creation. Her strong background in environmental studies and previous experience working on solar energy during Janet Napolitano's governorship in Arizona greatly influenced her focus on these issues. Mayor Gallego highlighted that her platform primarily revolves around safety, economic development, and a combination of sustainability and infrastructure.

She emphasized the importance of providing residents with the necessary tools to ensure their safety, whether it be protection from extreme heat, COVID-19, or violence. Additionally, Mayor Gallego stressed the significance of enabling people to earn a livable wage and support their families, emphasizing,

> Our residents need the tools to stay safe, whether it is from heat, COVID 19 or violence. We need to make sure people have the ability to earn a good living, to take care of their family. City of Phoenix provides everything from the transportation, the streets, to the water system on which we depend, we are a desert city, and we need to do it in a way that respects our natural environment and is sustainable.

To achieve success, particularly in a city as large as Phoenix with a population of 1.6 million residents (comparable to the size of some small countries), Mayor Gallego stressed the importance of collaboration between local officials, businesses, and communities. Moving beyond mere policy implementation, she emphasized the significance of targeted investments that incentivize action and align with desired outcomes.

In response to the challenges posed by the pandemic, local officials recognized the need to combine policy initiatives with strategic investments to support parents and children in navigating the constraints on livelihood and education. Mayor Gallego, reflecting on her role as mayor, aimed to draw from her own challenging experiences during the COVID-19 crisis to make impactful investments that would enhance the quality of life for all residents, particularly parents. One major area of investment focused on bridging the digital divide, ensuring that individuals had access to devices and connectivity.

Furthermore, Mayor Gallego's commitment to narrowing the digital divide was accompanied by the creation of a digital portal called the "Environment and Sustainability Information Hub," which was launched on Earth Day in early 2022. During the unveiling, she highlighted significant achievements, stating,

> This fiscal year, we have implemented an aggressive and accelerated Climate Action Plan, established the first-ever public Office of Heat Response and

Mitigation, piloted Cool Pavement technology, initiated the planting of the first Cool Corridor, invested in the Circular Economy, and introduced an Electric Vehicle Roadmap.[7]

These investments and initiatives showcased Mayor Gallego's dedication to addressing climate change and promoting sustainability in Phoenix. By proactively tackling issues such as heat response, circular economy practices, and electric vehicle adoption, she demonstrated her commitment to building a more resilient and sustainable city for the benefit of all residents.

INVITING EVERYONE TO THE PARTY TO LET THE GREEN TIMES ROLL

During the pandemic, two former members of the Global System for Mobile Communications Association (GSMA), Simon Hayman and Tom Chinnock, took the initiative to launch a series of conferences called "Tech for Climate Action" with a specific focus on technology's role in addressing climate imperatives. Their intentional approach was to bring together governmental entities, technology experts, and industry players (enterprises) to foster collaboration in tackling climate challenges. Their efforts garnered rapid engagement and support from various stakeholders. The first conference, held in Brussels in October 2022, featured speakers and attendees from the offices of the European Commission, secretaries of state, city mayors, parliamentary representatives, venture funders, and leaders from the transportation, energy, and technology sectors. Building on this success, their second conference took place in Washington DC in March 2023, where they once again achieved a similar level of multi-stakeholder engagement. These conferences served as platforms for productive private–public dialogues centered around technology and digital innovation enablers for climate action.

While it is impossible to definitively determine the level of success Hayman and Chinnock would have achieved in bringing together policymakers, private interests, and technology innovators on the topic of climate action before the pandemic, their ongoing series of conferences continues to gain momentum. These conferences serve as a platform to further advance the energy and focus that emerged as a result of the pandemic, as discussed throughout this book. The series has capitalized on the heightened awareness and urgency surrounding climate action, drawing upon the experiences and lessons learned during the pandemic. By fostering collaboration and dialogue among diverse stakeholders, Hayman and Chinnock's efforts contribute to the ongoing efforts to address climate challenges and drive sustainable innovation.

GOVERNANCE BALANCED BY BETTER HABITS

Governance plays a crucial role in driving the intensified sustainability efforts needed in the post-pandemic era, recognizing that sticks can be stronger motivators than carrots when it comes to human behavior. Regulations and rules are essential tools to encourage the desired authentic behavior and action. This governance should be established by national, international, regional, and industry bodies, ensuring a comprehensive approach.

Even if certain actions may initially lack substance, they have the power to initiate a shift in behavior. Through repetition, these behavioral changes can lead to the development of better habits over time. Such habits, when put into motion, can yield sustainable results that withstand the test of time and future challenges.

In our hyperconnected world, where communities are digitally interconnected, the impact of different regions will eventually balance out. Sharing and implementing best practices will raise the overall standard, benefiting countries around the globe that face the pressing challenges of climate change, social injustice, and pandemic-induced inequities. By working together, we can create a more sustainable and just future for all.

NOTES

1. Science Based Target Initiative. (2022, June). *SCIENCE-BASED NET-ZERO Scaling Urgent Corporate Climate Action Worldwide.* https://sciencebasedtargets.org/resources/files/SBTiProgressReport2021.pdf

2. Ashcroft, S. (2022, June 14). *EcoVadis Secures $500mn to Ramp-Up Sustainability Ratings.* Supply Chain. https://supplychaindigital.com/sustainability/ecovadis-secures-50mn-as-it-ramps-up-sustainability-ratings
3. Reference needed here.
4. Reference needed here
5. Reference needed here
6. Reference needed here
7. City of Phoenix. (2022, April 22). *Mayor Gallego Unveils Environment and Sustainability Information Hub.* Mayor's Office. https://www.phoenix.gov/newsroom/mayors-office/2349

4

Revisiting Risk and Revitalizing *Shareholder "Value"*

THE BUSINESS MEETS ITS (NEW) MAKER(S)

The phrase "When America sneezes, the world catches a cold" has long captured the influence of the United States as the leading global economic power, as measured by Gross Domestic Product (GDP). In 2021, US GDP stood at US$23 trillion, with China as the second-largest economy at US$18 trillion, and Japan ranking third at US$5 trillion. This expression originated from a similar phrase used in the 18th century, "When France sneezes the whole of Europe catches a cold," reflecting the dominance of French influence during that era.

However, the pandemic has potentially reshaped this phrase to "When any part of the interconnected global economy sneezes, the risk of a severe cold affects everyone." As we have explored in the preceding chapters, digital innovation has empowered communities to adapt and thrive, and leverage an increasing attention to social sustainability principles. The impact of this transformation extends even further for global businesses and industries, amplifying their role in shaping the interconnected economic landscape.

In fact, during the pandemic and in the coming years following, the "purpose" of business, and the drivers that inform or influence this purpose, will experience an irreversible paradigm shift—away from the definition of "value" based on pure profit to one that regards the impact to multiple stakeholders within and without the organization. As Larry Fink,

DOI: 10.4324/9781003462347-4

CEO of Blackrock, the largest private equity firm in the world with assets under management now at more than US$8 trillion (yes, trillion), wrote in his 2021 (with the pandemic in full swing) annual letter to CEOs globally:

I believe that the pandemic has presented such an existential crisis – such a stark reminder of our fragility – that it has driven us to confront the global threat of climate change more forcefully and to consider how, like the pandemic, it will alter our lives.

(bold font in the original letter)

Fink continued in his beseech to corporate leaders, "It has reminded us how the biggest crises, whether medical or environmental, demand a global and ambitious response."

In this segment, we examine the interplay between enterprise and the sustainability agenda, and how businesses have both contributed to and benefited from this transformative movement. We delve into the dynamics of social sustainability and its impact on corporate communities, customers, and the fundamental principles that drive businesses to not only survive but thrive in a new era of what can be defined as "growth."

As previously discussed, the pandemic highlighted the significant influence of community and grassroots movements on enterprise dynamics. They are the engines by which local and global communities thrive.

Businesses are essentially a reflection of the local and global communities they operate in, serving as the driving force behind their prosperity. Conversely, businesses rely heavily on stakeholder engagement and support from these communities to thrive. Community movements played and continue to play a pivotal role in shaping employees' influence within organizations toward sustainable practices. This influence ranges from increased scrutiny of an organization's climate change commitments to a heightened focus on essential principles of Diversity, Equity, and Inclusion (DEI) within the workplace.

Planet, Purpose, People

One of the notable shifts during the pandemic was the increased focus on the *human* aspect of "human resources" (HR), even as we have become desensitized to the word *human* in the title.

The global impact of COVID-19 compelled organizations to prioritize the health and well-being of their workforce, recognizing the importance of nurturing and retaining talent. Phrases like "Quiet Quitting" and the "Great Resignation" became common in the media, as employees reevaluated their career paths and positions within companies. With the intense competition for talent, particularly in the technology sector which thrived during the pandemic, corporations began placing greater emphasis and scrutiny on the "S" or social sustainability aspect of Environmental, Social, and Governance (ESG) considerations, particularly through DEI initiatives.

Forward-thinking organizations are increasingly realizing that the benefits of diversity cannot be measured solely by numbers. It goes beyond quotas; it strengthens the organizational culture, values, and overall health of the company. Steve Ramseur, former Chief Innovation Officer at JLL, eloquently captured this sentiment during our interview:

> In corporate America, we are obsessed with measurement. We measure everything, from the percentage of Hispanics to other metrics. But in doing so, we sometimes lose sight of the individual behind the numbers. We fail to see the beautiful human beings with their own lives and experiences.

Ramseur insisted,

> I look at the spreadsheet and I say, okay, the numbers are good. We must be doing a great job on our sustainability or on our DE& I. But then you go to the water cooler, you go to the water cooler, and you listen to the talk of those people who are disenfranchised, and they don't match the, they don't match the numbers.

Regrettably, in the pursuit of compliance and external pressures, there have been instances where organizations engage in tokenism, appointing underrepresented leaders merely to fulfill a checkbox requirement. The pandemic highlighted the risks of not prioritizing better practices around DEI. With the rise of remote work and increased reliance on video conferencing for communication and collaboration, the concept of "belonging" became closely associated with DEI in corporate talent discussions.

Using an oft-cited metaphor, diversity can be likened to receiving an invitation to the dance, inclusion is being invited to *participate* in the dance, and belonging is feeling connected and *engaged* with the music, enjoying the experience to the fullest extent.

NTT's Chief Marketing Officer, Vito Mabrucco, emphasized how the pandemic acted as a catalyst for magnifying existing inequalities. Movements like the Great Resignation disproportionately impacted women who shouldered most childcare responsibilities and were adversely affected by the closure of daycare centers and schools. The repercussions of this on diverse teams raised concerns for businesses. Mabrucco shared the story of his own mother who had lived in Canada for over 60 years but did not speak English, highlighting the importance of preserving diversity within the context of being an integral part of a larger whole. He stressed, "It's not just about our visible characteristics like race, gender, or sexual orientation. It's the amalgamation of our backgrounds and experiences that influence our actions and thoughts, shaping our interactions and bringing together different cultures."

The pandemic brought a sense of humanity into the corporate setting, as virtual platforms like Zoom and Teams allowed colleagues and leaders to enter each other's homes and vice versa. Along the way, amidst business discussions, we got to know our colleagues' children, spouses, and pets. Surprisingly unexpected interactions, such as a toddler appearing half-naked in the background, fostered stronger bonds with coworkers, customers, and partners, transcending differences of race, creed, or gender.

Mike Burns, of Burns Brothers who we met in an earlier chapter, bases his insights on diversity in part on his experience in Iraq, where for seven months he was head of civil–military operations in Northern Iraq at the request of US General David Petraeus. Working in Iraq, Burns said,

> I had to leverage people of all different backgrounds in order to accomplish things that had never been accomplished before. We had tasks that were very complex and very difficult. During those times, I absolutely saw the power of leveraging people's experiences and insight in order to accomplish something.

After his time in Iraq, Burns was asked to run diversity enrollment and recruiting at West Point.

> What the army had realized was that most of the officers in the Army were white males, and the majority of enlisted personnel were Brown and Black

people. The Army knew that if there wasn't a better balance, those who lead wouldn't necessarily truly understand those they were leading. So, they thought, if we get it right at West Point, we can get it right for the Army.

Burns went from West Point to Citi Group and then to Conduent. In each arena, he saw large organizations struggling to better appreciate the importance of diverse teams—internal or external. "What I recognized," Burns said, "is that it was all about people. It didn't matter about the industry, and it didn't matter about the environment. If you could really tap into, understand, and leverage people, then any organization can be successful." A lot of organizations struggle with that, he said. "I also saw that many organizations didn't really take time to understand people." From there his organization, Burns Brothers, was born. Burns and his brother—formerly a partner at a major DC law firm—work with organizations from the Fortune100 to nonprofits, and all sizes and sectors in between. Burns emphasized that every client they work with must share a common aspiration: the desire to foster genuine, sustainable, and impactful change by leveraging a deep understanding of the people they serve.

SOCIAL CAPITAL FOR SOCIAL SUSTAINABILITY

In the context of wealth gaps, "social capital" often remains an underestimated facet, particularly when examining gender disparities and the experiences of underrepresented groups. Social capital refers to the professional relationships we foster through social interactions. In the "old world" or the pre-pandemic era, this type of "power-networking" often occurred in traditional settings like golf courses, happy hours, or fraternity gatherings at universities—environments that were exclusive of classically underrepresented groups.

The rapid digitization that occurred during the pandemic, along with the closure of physical meeting spaces and the rise of virtual platforms, opened up new possibilities for greater democratization, and improved diversity in corporate leadership, particularly within boardrooms. As organizations embraced virtual interactions, it became easier to connect and collaborate with individuals from diverse backgrounds and perspectives.

This shift toward more diversified corporate boardrooms has led to a heightened awareness and consciousness toward ESG principles. With a broader range of voices and perspectives at the table, boardrooms are more inclined to consider the broader impact of their decisions on the environment, society, and corporate governance. This shift aligns with the growing recognition of the importance of sustainable and responsible business practices.

Lawrence Chu of Moelis noted that we have already seen a tremendous increase in ESG awareness over the past several years in the boardroom. "Since then," Chu said, "it's become much bigger—every board has an ESG section. Previously, this was normally rolled into the HR section. Now it's its own section; they spend a lot of time talking about it. They've set priorities." Chu went on to say that when he is involved in doing due diligence on other companies, ESG is one area where they now spend more time, "which is something that I've never done in my career prior to this."

Diversity on teams, in leadership, and the boardroom has been in a crucible for decades. And the focus on ESG has been a topic in the boardroom but has become notably pronounced as leaders became particularly attenuated to risk factors—especially given the multithreaded risk factors the pandemic introduced to the total business ecosystem.

In a study conducted by Harvard Law School on the presence of climate and diversity, equity and inclusion, an overwhelming majority of board directors indicated that including both items within a sustainability agenda is most commonly a focus for the entire board or, at minimum, assigned within a committee. Only 14% of boards indicated that they have no oversight on climate-related risks (see Figure 4.1).[1] And only 6% indicated they have no oversight on broader workforce DEI (Figure 4.2).

Sustainability and ESG have become an integral part of an organization's performance, risk management, and overall stewardship as a contributor to our collective ability to thrive.

EMPOWERING WOMEN AND ALLIES

Gavriella Schuster, former Corporate Vice President at Microsoft, described this long-standing opportunity to converge as a community,

Where does oversight of climate-related risks and opportunities primarily reside within your board?

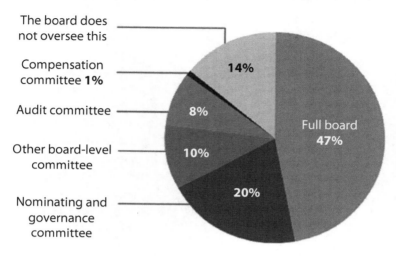

The board does not oversee this

Compensation committee **1%**

Audit committee — 8%

Other board-level committee — 10%

Nominating and governance committee

14%

Full board 47%

20%

FIGURE 4.1

Chart representing responses of where the oversight of climate-related risk sits within the corporate board

specifically in the technology industry. What she told us about her experiences will unfortunately be an all-too-common tale to other women who have worked in technology.

Schuster referenced how she was part of an email thread a few years ago among people in the technology industry sharing experiences and asking for advice, many of them "feeling like they were either stuck or in the wrong place." She noted the unexpectedly large number of women chiming in, noting, "There were maybe 30 people or so on the thread. As I was reading through it, my first reaction was, yes, I get it. I've experienced all those things." Schuster began reaching out to people she knew, "asking the questions, talking to them, coaching them, talking about what they could do, how they could think about it." But then, she said, "As I headed down that path, I had this 'Aha' moment where I thought, there are no men on this."

She continued, "It was like the men don't have the same experience. Every single one of these women asks, 'Is it me, or is there something else going on?' And as I reflected on that, I thought, there *is* something else going on." As Schuster realized, even after 30 years, "a lot of these behaviors and these microaggressions still occur, and we need to do something about

Where does oversight of broader workforce diversity, equity and inclusion primarily reside within your board?

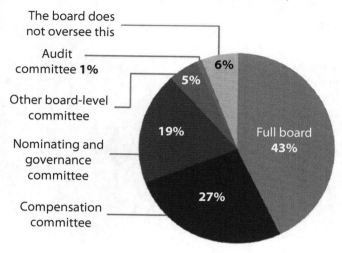

The board does not oversee this

Audit committee **1%**

Other board-level committee

Nominating and governance committee

Compensation committee

6%

5%

19%

Full board **43%**

27%

FIGURE 4.2

Chart representing responses of where the oversight of DEI in the workforce sits within the corporate board

it. And then I was like, oh, my gosh, I'm a Corporate Vice President ... I think I need to do something about it." She recalled,

> I realized that I had really become numb to a lot of these situations over the years, but these microaggressions didn't bother me. And it was wrong that they didn't bother me. I realized that if I wasn't making a point to address them, then I was being a lousy role model.

Schuster continued,

> If other women in my team or around me saw that happening, they'd go, "Well, if Gavriella doesn't do something or say something, how could I?" So, I realized that I had a responsibility to be very active on this and figure out how to be a better role model and how to be a better ally.

Schuster noted that part of remembering our humanity is fighting against those microaggressions and ensuring that the technology ecosystem is an inclusive and welcoming place. And Schuster was able to share strategies from her own experience that help make that possible. "As I started thinking," Schuster said, "I realized I was building allies." She explained,

> If I was in a group of people where I felt like something was kind of toxic, or I couldn't be my authentic self, or I was getting dismissed or disrespected, I would build allies within that group. That would give me more of a platform to be empowered and to really participate and contribute. And I found that to be very effective.

Schuster clarified that this approach was especially helpful in certain groups, such as,

> If one of the people just felt like, well, "Women don't have a place here, I don't even know why you're here." I had another ally who recognized that I was constantly interrupted or that my ideas weren't being taken seriously. They were able to say something like, "Oh, actually, I don't know if Gavriella was quite done" or "Gavriella, do you want to finish your thought?" or, "Hey, Joe, that's a really great idea; I think it's very similar to what Gavriella just said" or "Gavriella, do you want to share more about that? Give us a little bit more context."

Being an ally in the way that Schuster describes is not a heavy lift, but it can make a significant the difference to someone else.

Schuster distinguished between the quality of *diversity* and the action of *inclusion*. She confided,

> I realized it's not enough just to hire for diversity. You have to have an inclusive environment. If you don't, then it doesn't matter how much diversity you have. You're not going to realize the benefits—the innovation, the better decision-making, the increased profitability. You're not going to get to a level of retention of the diverse people that you've hired because they're just going to feel like "I don't belong here."

During the pandemic, organizations faced a dual talent management challenge that further magnified the importance of DEI. On one hand, unemployment rates unexpectedly dropped, creating a highly competitive hiring landscape. Simultaneously, employees embarked on a trend of "quiet quitting," seeking new opportunities and leaving their current positions. This posed a significant challenge for enterprises, particularly in industries requiring diverse leadership and team growth. They had to intensify their efforts to attract and hire top talent while also focusing on retaining their existing teams to minimize disruptions and address the "quiet quitting" phenomenon.

MAKING IT, AND KEEPING IT, REAL

As expected, sustainability has become a prominent topic in corporate boardrooms, exerting a significant influence on the direction and actions of corporations. In a report titled "Key Trends That Will Drive the ESG Agenda in 2022," S&P Global highlights that corporate boards and government leaders will face mounting pressure to demonstrate their ability to understand and oversee a range of ESG issues, including climate change, human rights, and social unrest.

The values held by corporate boards are also undergoing transformation due to these factors. Jennifer Cohen, representing Toyota, observed that boards are now engaging in discussions about diverse stakeholders, recognizing that the focus extends beyond shareholders' financial interests. Cohen said, "I am hearing boards talk a lot more about different stakeholders—not just the shareholders making money, although that's a huge part—but being more cognizant that there are other stakeholders than just the people who are holding shares." She emphasized that these changes would not have occurred without the catalyst of the pandemic. It is crucial to view these shifts as interconnected, rather than isolated checkboxes. Cohen emphasized that sustainability, diversity, and equity and inclusion are all intertwined in this new landscape.

Jenifer Rogers is a senior corporate leader who serves on multiple public company boards in Japan. She noted the difference this shift in ethos makes toward meaningful change, marking how organizations will prosper in the post-pandemic new world order. The Japan Corporate Governance Code's revision in 2021 led to promoting more women and foreign directors to boards, as well as more ESG reporting. The governance piece pushes companies to have more women in middle management, to fill the pipeline to upper management. Though unfortunately that enforcement must come through policy and regulation, which have been increasing in various regions throughout the pandemic and beyond, it's the kind of tail that will need to wag the dog for the momentum to move in the right direction.

Despite some progress, there is still a considerable journey ahead to achieve significant change. A study by Harvard Law School revealed that in 2021, the global average of women on corporate boards stood at 19.7%, reflecting a mere increase of 2.8% since the previous report in 2019. At this pace, achieving gender parity in boardrooms will not be realized until 2045. However, as organizations face increasing demands for disclosure and transparency, there is hope that this growth will accelerate. By integrating social sustainability efforts with environmental sustainability imperatives, we can foster the innovation necessary to drive meaningful change and progress.

INSIDE OUT

In today's business landscape, environmental impact, social equity, and good governance have become essential pillars embedded within the DNA of a high-performing culture. The concept of Corporate Social Responsibility (CSR) reports, which used to be a mere box to check for many corporations, has evolved significantly. The pandemic has prompted global organizations to create or accelerate their sustainability ambitions, driven by the growing influence of employee agency within an organization.

As Jennifer Cohen from Toyota highlighted, it is no longer sufficient to solely focus on diverse boards. Sustainability governance, both for customers and partners, as well as within internal teams, should be considered. This pressure for sustainable practices stems not only from customers but also from future employees. The younger generations, such as Generation Z and soon Generation Alpha, are conducting thorough evaluations of potential employers and rejecting internship and job offers from organizations that do not align with their sustainability values. This shift in mindset reflects the increasing importance of sustainability as a deciding factor in choosing where to work and contribute their skills.

Cohen emphasized, "I'm hearing about ESG in so many different places. People are talking about sustainability in the environment. Because of COVID, they're talking about sustainability of talent." There is a growing awareness that corporate engagement needs to include all these different pieces around social sustainability—in combination with the hyper focus on environmental sustainability. As Cohen put it, "I don't want to lose what we're seeing in terms of how we manage talent and diversity and how we talk about equity and social justice or lose it in relation to sustainability and the environment."

Alison Taylor runs a think tank called Ethical Systems, teaches at the NYU Stern School of Business, and is a senior advisor at BSR (Business for Social Responsibility)—a sustainable business network and consultancy focused on creating a world where we all thrive on this healthy spaceship. According to Taylor,

> The biggest story of the pandemic has really been employee activism and business leaders focusing on employees—on what employees think, on what employees want, on how employees want their companies to show up in terms of ethics and values.

Taylor noted this was especially true in highlighting differences in employee protections and benefits, between both white-collar and blue-collar workers, and American and European employees. "There was a lot of focus on the exploitation of delivery workers, gig workers, and so on in the US," she said.

> Then a lot of focus on which companies do and don't provide health care, do and don't provide sick leave—all these very critical, fundamental rights. If you're European like me, you sort of take these for granted, but you can't take them for granted in the US. There's been a lot more focus on the human side of ESG and less of this being seen as a technical environmental discipline.

In this way, Taylor says, corporate ESG forces have been rising from within the walls of enterprise. People are watching how companies respond. "The big story for me since the beginning of the pandemic has been the rise of employee voice and employee power. I think that's not going away."

Ultimately, how corporations think about "human" resources is shifting and becoming more embedded within the broader sustainability context, and the name of the HR department is changing. The Chief Human Resources Officer (CHRO) is now "Chief People Officer" and "Chief

Talent Officer." The one-way "resource" stance of humans has evolved, and accelerated during the pandemic, to a symbiotic, and two-way, exchange of value for Enterprise, Inc.

---

50 SHADES OF "IN THE OFFICE"

Brent Waechter, senior IT manager at Toyota Motor North America, provided valuable insights into the people aspect of the sustainability agenda, focusing specifically on the impact of remote work. Waechter spoke about how in his career in corporate IT, it was not uncommon to see people spending more time in hotel rooms than at home. When the pandemic started, Waechter was in a business operations role with Toyota and the change was striking. The mandate came down: "We'll rotate the team to reduce the number of people in the office," he said, "And so I left thinking I was coming back in a couple of days, and I haven't been back in two years." Initially, the mandate was to rotate teams to reduce office occupancy, and what was expected to be a temporary arrangement turned into an extended period of remote work spanning two years.

Waechter talked about how he had to help the organization navigate that transition to supporting people remotely, beyond just functional administration.

> From an IT perspective, we had to figure out how to support people technologically. But the other interesting part was how do we support our people emotionally and socially. How do we make sure people feel appreciated, feel connected, and support existing relationships.

Waechter detailed steps aimed at making otherwise impersonal virtual interactions more personal. "This means increased email communication from our leaders, small, recorded videos from our leaders to make it more personal," and even appearances from kitchen tables—little things aimed at emphasizing shared humanity.

The shift to remote work during the pandemic brought about an interesting dynamic of both equalizing and highlighting the digital divide in our work experiences. While the mode of communication became standardized for everyone, with laptops, microphones, desks, and chairs, it also revealed disparities in access to optimal equipment, reliable bandwidth, and dedicated workspace.

As Brent Waechter pointed out, the challenge was to find ways to address our innate need for connection while ensuring productivity. It became apparent that not everyone had the privilege of a suitable remote work environment. Some individuals faced limitations due to the size and configuration of their homes, lacking the resources to create an ideal workspace.

This disparity underscored the importance of finding inclusive solutions that accommodate diverse circumstances. It prompted organizations to consider how to support employees who may face challenges in achieving an optimal remote work setup. By acknowledging these disparities and working toward equitable solutions, we can foster a more inclusive and supportive work environment for all.

BUSINESS OF THE PEOPLE, FOR THE PEOPLE

During our conversation, Mary De Wysocki, Chief Sustainability Officer at Cisco, highlighted the increased engagement and emotional connection to work that has emerged through hybrid work arrangements. She emphasized the significance of having executive teams virtually present in employees' homes through platforms like Webex and other remote meeting technologies.

This shift has leveled the playing field for workers of diverse backgrounds, including race, gender, culture, and age. Remote work has fostered deeper emotional connections and provided opportunities to take pride in one's work while empathizing with colleagues who were previously less accessible. De Wysocki shared a notable experience from that week, when a 65-year-old man joined her team with a clear declaration of enthusiasm: "This is what I want to do!"

According to De Wysocki, this emotional commitment fuels a sense of magic within the workforce. It applies to employees of all ages, as people yearn to be recognized and be part of something meaningful. The younger generation, in particular, is often more attuned to the importance of values and passion in their work. De Wysocki observed that young individuals "feel it, see it, and have more willingness to take action," but this sentiment resonates across age groups and diverse backgrounds.

The pandemic created very raw moments in all our lives—whether from being very present to illness and possibly even death, to the stress of a packed multi-generational house, to losing a job. So many unprecedented disruptions occurred in our lives with no sense of when things might "normalize." It was a remarkable time of vulnerability and uncertainty that had many of us recalibrate our purpose and our values. People all want to be part of something meaningful. COVID-19 forced organizations to recognize the humanity of their workforce and prioritize people, and to be present to the emotional entanglements of hybrid work or work-from-home positions, and the emotional triggers of pride and empathy.

ESG Takes Its Gloves Off

While the heartbeat of organizations, the employees, took on new energy around the S in ESG, enterprises also responded to pressures from customers and other external ecosystems around sustainability demands. Tonie Hansen was Senior Director of CSR and Sustainability at NVIDIA at the time of our research, which has similarly given her a first-hand view of how corporate engagement with ESG is changing. She told us,

> For the past 16 years, I've been embedding different environmental, social, and even sometimes governance elements into the company's overall business operations as we go—whether it's diversity and inclusion, strengthening our supplier responsibility program, sustainability, or charitable giving. More recently, this has included working with external stakeholders, such as investors, to make sure they understand the strength that we have as a company, how we take feedback into consideration, and how we weave our products and operations into an overall story that talks about creating a resilient company.

That trend accelerated drastically during the pandemic. Companies became more aware of how they needed to step up not just for Black customers and employees after George Floyd's death, but for underserved populations in general. Hansen explained, "This is not only about bringing in a more diverse audience, but what is the environment that we're creating for that community as well? Do they feel safe? It seems many tech companies kicked that off during that time."

The pandemic shed a spotlight on climate change, prompting a broader recognition of its importance. Hansen highlighted the significant impact of the State of the Climate in 2020 report by the World Meteorological Organization, which delivered alarming findings on the consequences of climate change. This report served as a wake-up call for companies, compelling them to take action. Hansen emphasized that the warnings in the report propelled companies and investors to demand more comprehensive sustainability efforts.

The expectations for companies have evolved beyond simply reducing their carbon footprint within their own operations. They are now expected to take responsibility for their entire value chain, finance sustainability initiatives, track progress, and minimize their environmental impact as much as possible. Any remaining emissions should be offset through appropriate measures.

The pandemic has brought these issues to the forefront, making the message even more urgent. Corporate Social Responsibility has taken on a new level of importance, closely tied to the success and long-term viability of businesses.

The movement toward business and enterprise accountability, encompassing a broader set of stakeholders and considering environmental and social concerns, gained significant traction prior to the pandemic. In August 2019, the Business Roundtable made a landmark declaration, stating that the purpose of a corporation extends beyond maximizing shareholder value to also include creating value for employees, customers, suppliers, and communities.

As the pandemic unfolded and various events and movements highlighted the importance of sustainability, encompassing areas such as climate change and social equity, the prominence of B-corps grew. B-corps, although still for-profit entities, prioritize not only profit but also environmental and social standards. These standards are verified by B Lab, a governing body. Since its establishment in 2006, over 5,000 organizations have received B-corp certification, with 1,000 of them certified in 2022 during the pandemic.

The pandemic period witnessed an acceleration of B-corps as consumers increasingly sought out businesses with sustainability designations. For some brands, having B-corp status has become a compelling selling point, as mentioned in the section on community movements. Moreover, even beyond B-corps, there is a growing expectation that brands will strive for greater equity, improve their supply chains, and take a stand for human rights.

Good for Me, Good for You, Good for All of Us

Sustainability has shifted from being a "cost" to an opportunity, and in many industries an imperative to being successful and competitive. Tenneco Senior Vice President and Chief ESG Officer Kim Yapchai noted this succinctly. She explained that she sees her role with ESG as coming down to this: "What's the right thing to do, AND what's going to make our company perform better and be stronger." Compliance is indisputably a part of that, but it includes more. Each year Ethisphere produces a list of the world's most ethical companies—and then charts those companies' performances against the large cap index. As Yapchai noted, "There's a 25% gap between the two. The world's most ethical company winners are performing better than the rest." Why such a difference in performance? She tactfully mused: "It's because you're not damaging your brand."

Bracken Darrell, former CEO of Logitech and current CEO of VF Corp (the parent company of notable brands like The North Face, Dickies, Vans, and more), approached the topic from a different perspective but arrived at the same conclusion: companies that embrace ESG principles drive greater innovation, and the market rewards this innovation. During our conversation, we discussed the emerging SEC metrics for ESG compliance, and Darrell shared his viewpoint. He expressed, "I believe it's ultimately about profits, and I might be in a slightly different camp than most people on this matter. I don't think the solution lies in a balanced scorecard or abandoning the focus on profits for companies."

According to Darrell, "we (enterprise) won't have a choice." Companies will not have an alternative; customers will not allow it. He explained,

> I don't see this as a noble act on the part of companies or investors to declare that profits are no longer the sole measure of success. It is a result of the forces of humanity driving this change. The companies that get on board are going to be rewarded, either because they're more innovative and innovation wins, or because customers and consumers want that. If you're a corporate customer, you're going to say, "Yes, give me this choice between a company that's carbon neutral or climate positive and one that's not and all things created equal?" It's a no brainer.

As Darrell underscored the handsome rewards:

> The good news is this just simply aligns corporate success and return on shareholder investment with DEI and environmental sustainability, so I don't think it's a big sacrifice. I can almost guarantee you that the companies that get on board first will be rewarded handsomely for what they do.

Fundamentally, organizations need to adopt practices, goals and processes that drive dramatic improvement with sustainability NOT as an "add on" but to fundamentally driving the business. This habit will drive businesses, especially for those that lead the way.

Luis Neves, CEO of the Global Enabling Sustainability Initiative (GeSI), comes from an extended background in ICT as well as in politics, and had similar insights.

> There are social and environmental dimensions of sustainability, but you cannot run a business if you do not make profits. So I always looked at sustainability as a key driver of profitability. My main challenge when I started to work on sustainability was to explain that sustainability was not a problem, it was a solution.

Neves explained that when he was first working on sustainability initiatives at T-Mobile, it was much less a part of the corporate landscape. "Sustainability was very much about communicating good projects on the company toward the society, but not really looking into the core dimension of what sustainability means in terms of integrating sustainable mindset to the different operations of the company."

As many of us have likely noticed in our own work, Neves noted sustainability ultimately or primarily should start with top management and then cascade down to different areas of the company. He made it his mission

> to bring all those dimensions into product development, procurement, marketing, sales, different operations, efficiencies in buildings and data centers. I always try to look at sustainability as a key driver of improving company performance in areas where people were not looking.

However, he faced challenges when top leadership focused on short-term return on investment instead of considering long-term impact. This created a dilemma as sustainability sometimes hindered their ability to achieve quick targets and reap immediate rewards. Neves often found himself perceived as a showstopper, as he encountered resistance in bringing sustainability into the company's mindset. Neves acknowledged that the tide has markedly turned, and quite energetically amidst the pandemic.

Roli Agrawal is Chief of Staff to the Global CEO at NTT DATA Inc. She shared that her organization is prioritizing ESG progress "because yes, it's the right thing to do, but at the same time it makes a lot more business sense as well to focus on sustainability and on diversity." Even Amazon, she said, has embraced the change, noting how their packaging changed significantly during the pandemic to cut down on waste and extra packaging materials. Customers notice this, which engenders loyalty, which in turn, enhances the bottom line. Companies might want to go that route from a profit perspective, Agrawal noted, but in doing so, "they are making customers more happy and more loyal," and that in turn drives more traffic and sales—and the virtuous wheel of value turns.

As sustainability and ESG have become deeply ingrained in the mainstream mindset, particularly accelerated by the pandemic, the notion of a tradeoff between pursuing sustainability and achieving profitability has significantly diminished. In fact, business prosperity and sustainability have now become inseparable, like two intertwined components of a single entity. They are no longer separate entities where one can shift without affecting the other. Instead, they have merged into an alloy, where the success of one is intrinsically tied to the success of the other.

HEADSPACE FOR SUSTAINABLE INNOVATION

Rachel Payne is a multi-faceted professional, holding various roles such as Managing Director, Head of ESG, Impact and Origination at FullCycle, Chair, Founder & CEO at FEM, and Senior Program Officer at Google.org. Her diverse experience provides her with a comprehensive perspective on sustainability and its impact on businesses. During the COVID-19 pandemic, when traditional business practices were disrupted, Payne observed a need for reevaluation across all aspects of work, noting,

During COVID, when business as usual was completely upended, people were forced to reorganize everything from the way they do their work to the nature of their work. They had to pull back, especially with the disruption of supply chains, which gave space and time for a rethink of everything.

One of the things observed when working at Nike was that there's a lot that can be done. How you make a product and the materials used in a product can lead to better or worse levels of sustainability. What was becoming more and more evident is it's also about corporate supply chains because that's what's ultimately going to influence 90% of emissions levels. This notion of holding large multinational corporations accountable for their supply chains became a theme that was reinforced with numerous analysts and other folks who are beginning to really look at ESG as a lens for risk, because the disruption of supply chains during COVID highlighted how generally vulnerable supply chains were.

Payne noted those disruptions have made us all more familiar with the sort of global risk factors that could further disrupt performance.

That's a major move for institutionalizing climate reporting in a way that's consistent, but also gives potential investors and existing shareholders an opportunity to understand the full set of risk factors. Even moving beyond climate as a risk, there's also the notion of value creation in ESG. Many companies like Nike and others are now trying to compete against their peers by demonstrating more sustainable practices.

The pandemic has proliferated a sustainable innovation mindset more than ever, and corporations are at the heart of how all this ties meaningfully to economic growth.

ON PURPOSE

As observed in earlier chapters, companies that prioritized the well-being of their employees, adopted an ecosystem-focused approach to their supply chain, and practiced good governance were better equipped to manage risks during the pandemic, leading to improved performance. In fact, many of these companies outperformed those that did not prioritize sustainability. This trend caught the attention of investors, who sought out funds associated with ESG criteria as the pandemic ended.

This shift in corporate engagement has set off a cycle where sustainable organizations have a greater capacity for innovation, customer attraction, and investor appeal, ultimately leading to enhanced profitability. When executed effectively, this creates a virtuous feedback loop.

In the early days of the sustainability movement, the term "people, planet, and profit," coined by John Elkington in 1994, gained popularity. Shell's first sustainability report in 1997 incorporated this triple bottom line concept. In the post-pandemic era, another crucial "p" electrified the corporate sustainability landscape: purpose. Purpose surfaced repeatedly in our interviews, and it serves as the differentiating factor between sustainability initiatives that genuinely succeed and those that merely engage in greenwashing or fulfill legal obligations. Without allowing people to understand and align with their purpose, the concepts of people, planet, and profits lose their significance. Meaningful engagement cannot occur without purpose as the driving force for action.

When organizations embrace a clear purpose, they can engage with stakeholders in a more impactful manner. They can align themselves with movements that resonate with their purpose and develop related goals that weave together into a cohesive fabric of outcomes. Focusing solely on profit as the bottom line, without a larger purpose, results in missing out on the greater potential for total impact.

There are many ways to frame purpose. Mani Balakrishnan is Director of Sustainability & Social Responsibility at Zebra Technologies—where they use three 'I' words as their frame: inclusive, innovative, and impactful. "That really describes our philosophy at Zebra," Balakrishnan noted, "We want to win with inclusive, innovative and impactful behaviors." He explained that inclusive means not just representation, but also "making sure that people's ideas are heard. We want to be inclusive of ideas, inclusive of people—including representation." Innovative people bring innovation to the company, but Balakrishnan says there is more to it than that: "Impact is where people have to understand how my innovations, or my actions are impacting the broader society and the environment directly or indirectly. Once they understand or create that awareness, they will figure out how they can mitigate that."

Balakrishnan acknowledged that the final piece can be the most difficult. "We're so focused on the immediate gain that we sort of sometimes forget the big picture. We try to use that framing to look at ESG when we review actions and use that to mitigate our impact or amplify it in a positive way."

As we gradually recover from the impact of COVID-19 and reflect on its aftermath, there has been a collective reassessment on various levels—from individuals to families, communities, enterprises, and even nation states—regarding the underlying purpose behind our initiatives, actions, and ideas. The simplistic and binary approach of solely pursuing economic growth as a guiding principle for human endeavors has been disrupted by the profound impact of the pandemic and a growing awareness of our interdependence. This has sparked a wave of new perspectives and a revived emphasis on the importance of purpose over profit. We now recognize that our actions should be driven by a deeper understanding of why we do what we do. As we move forward, the hope is that this positive momentum continues, creating a sustained cycle of progress and fostering a world where purposeful endeavors thrive. Purpose over profit. Let's hope now is that this flywheel continues.

Risk and Compliance Look Good in Green

The pandemic served as a magnifying lens, exposing vulnerabilities within organizations and industries throughout their lifecycle. Shivam Kishore, from the UN, aptly described this complex reality, commenting

> We are talking about a very complex world. I started to see even in the management consulting businesses, where organizations are starting to think about how we ensure a bit more resiliency in the supply chain, so we are not over-reliant on a particular OEM or particular geography. How do we create a bit more resiliency to make sure certain geographies are impacted because of the supply chain function?

From his perspective the spotlight on supply chains became a catalyst for sustainability discussions, encompassing worker rights and environmental considerations.

Regulations aimed at promoting sustainability are also emerging, with a particular emphasis on supply chains. Initiatives such as Europe's Circular Economy action plan and sustainable product regulations focus on the supply chain perspective. For instance, in the European Union, upcoming regulations will require digital product passports for batteries and textiles, facilitating better product management and waste reduction. This approach highlights the intriguing connection between sustainability and supply chains, as efforts to enforce responsible practices and to minimize waste originate from this standpoint. It presents a compelling angle to consider when exploring sustainability in a broader context.

Phillippe Cases, co-founder and CEO of Topio Networks, echoed Kishore's point that sustainability equates to simple corporate risk management. He, too, put this in the context of supply chains—in one of the lessons of the pandemic, corporations are bringing more of the supply chain stateside (for American companies) or limiting them to Europe (for European companies) to hopefully lessen pandemic disruption.

Cases went on to say that the principle applies in several contexts.

> They want to do that because they realized by creating that global infra-structure, you're increasing risks, such as pandemic risks. So, the finance teams are looking now at pandemics and sustainability in the same level as risk. They are asking, "What are the risks that you're taking? Are you taking any pandemic risks? Are you taking any sustainability risks? And if you're taking those risks, what are they?"

Cases also noted that as governments become more stringent in expectations of sustainability with fines and other consequences, that changes the risk-reward calculus. "COVID is changing the mentality in terms of public–private partnership, in terms of understanding of risk, in terms of understanding of constraints," he said, and the same applies to the larger concept of corporate sustainability. Choosing less sustainable options may come with greater immediate profit rewards, but the risk is also greater depending on how stakeholders respond.

The role that the pandemic played in the magnification of corporate risk was key to how the sustainability agenda became a business imperative, and an indicator of the value of an organization. Nothing was more disruptive and exposed risk in the near term more than the pandemic, and in many ways sustainability issues are also materially tied to risk—even if on a longer-term horizon. This is why funds that were tagged with "ESG" had increased appeal during and post-pandemic. It was not about investors looking to invest in "Do Good," but rather to those companies that would have healthier prospects due to mitigation of risk from such disruptions as climate change, energy conservation, and social inequity unrest. We explore this in the next chapter.

When community, enterprise, and industries come together with a shared purpose, remarkable achievements can be accomplished. The development and rapid deployment of mRNA vaccines to combat COVID-19 exemplify the power of collaboration and scientific breakthroughs. While the research behind mRNA vaccines had been ongoing, the urgency of the pandemic propelled organizations and researchers to unite and prioritize this innovative solution. Federal funding and grants played a crucial role in expediting the process.

The extraordinary speed at which the vaccine was developed and distributed showcased the potential of aligning efforts across sectors. It begs the question of whether we, as a global society and community, can recognize the severity of other existential threats such as climate change and social inequity. Just like the pandemic, these challenges require swift action and collective engagement.

We now have the opportunity to harness the momentum generated by community involvement, investment, and corporate commitment to overcome seemingly insurmountable obstacles. By aligning our efforts and resources, we can address these pressing sustainability issues.

Disclosures for Better or ~~Worse~~ Even Better

Increased ESG disclosures rules have become instrumental in managing risk. The closer that senior leaders and corporate boards can correlate the risk management to better business, the more likelihood for success of adoption.

Xavier Denoly, the senior sustainability leader at Schneider we met in an earlier chapter, noted we have made huge leaps from where we were even ten years ago. Denoly looked at this from a decarbonization perspective. "Let's say ten years ago the big motive was to reduce your electricity bill by improving the energy efficiency. What happened is we gradually established a direct link between electricity usage and CO_2 emissions."

But we all know we can continually push for more incremental improvements now, and stakeholders do precisely that. "If you want to transform gradually," Denoly said, "do a better job at first electrifying everything that can be electrified—getting rid of other sources of energy that might be very harmful, for global warming or for the environment." Next, he continued, "If you go even deeper using the latest technologies to be able to have the best electrical energy efficiency, then you will reduce your consumption." And finally, he reiterated, "As much as possible, organize the switch to renewable types of energies."

This transparency of metrics and efforts started from voluntary motions and is increasingly being driven by compliance requirements. Fortunately, standards bodies and frameworks we reviewed in the earlier chapters have been instrumental in the innovative new value creation sought by companies all over the world. They help showcase ESG disclosure, transparency, and the strides companies are making toward greater sustainability. Collaboration and community building with these standards bodies can be a competitive advantage, not just in marketing but also in crafting better products.

Disclosure can put both internal and external pressure on companies and motivate improvement. Christine Tiballi, CEO and founder of DirtSat, cautioned that the enthusiasm and authenticity of intention is uneven. She pointed out,

> There are managers of big international funds saying, "Absolutely, we're going to be changing our tune. We're going to be divesting from possible fuels." Then the boards come in later and say, "Yeah, we're not really doing that." So, there's a real fight right now. People really want to make big changes, but it's a harder route to fully divest. I understand that will take more time than we want. But at the same time, I feel like there's a very big push and pull. There are people who really want to do the right thing.

Tiballi concluded,

> Pushing the SEC's new modeling of targets on financial disclosures is a really good first step, but there's a little bit of pushback from people who don't necessarily want to push this agenda as quickly as the rest of us would like.

INDUSTRY AND ENTERPRISE AS THE FUTURE-FORWARD STEWARD

Enterprise as we know it has a rich history spanning over 3,000 years, with its roots in ancient India and China. During this time, the foundations of modern business practices were laid, including the establishment of contracts, property ownership, and the formation of organizational structures. In the 1500s, government-backed companies like the Dutch East India Company emerged, fueling the expansion of global trade, and setting the stage for a global economy.

The pace of progress of economic growth accelerated massively during the industrial revolution in the 1800s, when innovation in process and automation fed an ever-faster machine of enterprise. All of this, in turn, transformed the planetary equilibrium, which we enjoyed as a race for thousands of years. Within a generation, we moved from this equilibrium period, or the Holocene geologic era, to the Anthropocene, where the very drivers of growth and notion of "progress" were directly impacting the very ecosystem of how the planet, people, and business thrive—"anthropo" for a human-defined and designed geologic age (see Figure 4.3).[2]

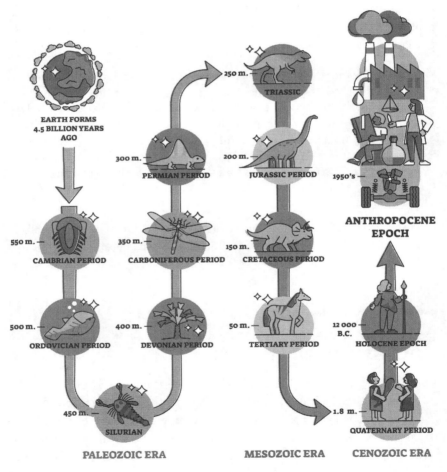

FIGURE 4.3
Historical narrative of the transitions to geological eras of planet Earth

The COVID-19 pandemic served as a stark reminder of the interconnectivity of the global economy and amplified awareness of the profound impact of business on various sustainability issues. It became evident that corporations have a crucial role to play in shifting from being part of the problem to becoming part of the solution. There is a pressing responsibility for businesses to address biodiversity loss, transition to sustainable energy sources, mitigate climate change, promote social equity, and contribute positively to the SDGs. By embracing this responsibility, corporations can be engines of the solution, as opposed to the source and accelerator of the risks that ultimately affect us all.

NOTES

1. Ashley, J., & Val Morrison, R. (2021, November 10). *ESG Governance: Board and Management Roles & Responsibilities.* Harvard Law School. https://corp-gov.law.harvard.edu/2021/11/10/esg-governance-board-and-management-roles-responsibilities/
2. *Anthropocene Epoch as Human Era in Global Geological Timeline Scale Outline Diagram* [Diagram]. (2021). Retrieved June 1, 2023 from https://www.istockphoto.com/vector/anthropocene-epoch-as-human-era-in-global-geological-timeline-outline-diagram-gm1346340523-424138375

5

Industrialization of Sustainability

CENTS AND SUSTAINABILITY

Investing in sustainability has been around for a few decades (Figure 5.1).[1] As mentioned in the chapter on corporate impact and influence, a prevailing perspective used to be that "ethical" or sustainability initiatives within a business were a cost center (and hence detrimental to the bottom-line and performance of a business). Now, sustainability has gained prominence within the investment community and strategies have evolved to focus on maximizing risk-adjusted returns rather than solely on ethical considerations.

Research, such as the study published in 2016 called "ESG Shareholder Engagement and Downside Risk"[2] delineated how engaging in Environmental, Social, and Governance (ESG) practices can reduce risks as well as provide insights into factors that may deleteriously affect a business. In 2017 (again, pre-pandemic), McKinsey published a report called *From Why to Why Not: Sustainable Investing as the New Normal*, from their private equity and investors practice group. The report set out to highlight the ways in which factors in ESG are, in fact, drivers of value. The report cites that more than one-quarter of global assets under management are being invested with the expectation that they are ESG are directly tied to a company's performance and subsequent market value.[3]

These studies demonstrate the evolution of ESG considerations in investment strategies, moving beyond solely ethical concerns to encompass risk management and financial performance. By acknowledging the value

DOI: 10.4324/9781003462347-5

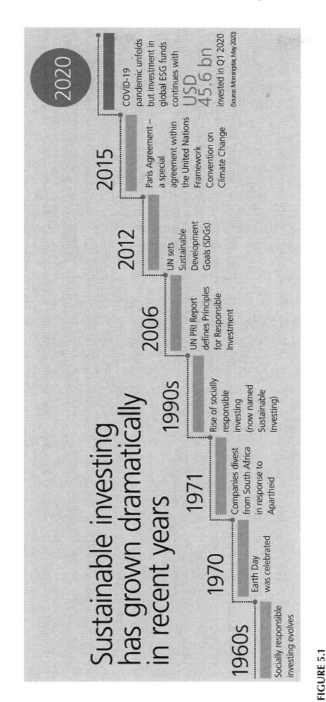

FIGURE 5.1

Growth in sustainability-related investments between the 1960s and 2020

of sustainable practices, investors can align their portfolios with companies that not only generate strong returns but also exhibit responsible and sustainable business practices. This shift reflects a growing recognition that sustainable investments can deliver both financial gains and positive societal and environmental impact.

A year into the pandemic, Blackrock CEO Larry Fink wrote in his annual CEO letter:

> It's been two years since I wrote that climate risk is investment risk. And in that short period, we have seen a tectonic shift of capital. Sustainable investments have now reached $4 trillion. Actions and ambitions towards decarbonization have also increased. This is just the beginning – the tectonic shift towards sustainable investing is still accelerating. Whether it is capital being deployed into new ventures focused on energy innovation, or capital transferring from traditional indexes into more customized portfolios and products, we will see more money in motion.[4]

That a prominent industry leader and corporate CEO who oversees investments of several billions of US dollars is focusing on sustainability investing should give many of us hope and give the VCs and entrepreneurs among us inspiration. It highlights the increasing importance and viability of sustainable investing in shaping the future of the global economy.

THE PANDEMIC PUT RISK CONSIDERATIONS ON STEROIDS

The impact of the COVID-19 pandemic on global economies was unparalleled, surpassing even the magnitude of the 2008 financial crisis. As the pandemic unfolded in early 2020, financial markets experienced a steep downturn, reminiscent of the Great Depression. The crisis exposed various risks, ranging from vulnerabilities in the supply chain to strains on healthcare systems and the rapid transition to remote work. In this environment, the significance of sustainability as a critical factor in investment decisions became even more pronounced.

As Philippe Cases from Topio Networks explained,

> In traditional finance theory, the more risk you take, the more potential reward. For the last fifty years, companies have ripped the reward of

globalization without properly assessing risks such as pandemics and climate change risks, whose disruptive impacts are meaningful. Now that the risks have materialized, people are considering which type of globalization they want to engage in. The impact of this change of perception hasn't been factored into asset prices.

If the focus on ESG and sustainability factors was big before, the pandemic certainly intensified the magnification.

Corporate Skin in the Sustainability Venture Game

Jim Adler of Toyota Ventures provided a corporate venture capitalist's take on the pragmatic pursuit of near-term revenues. He noted there is a far greater risk for brands to *not* invest in technology and innovation. It is far better business for Toyota's venture fund to fund investment in technologies in which they may not themselves be working, because those technologies may come into play in ways that are unknown today, but remarkably pertinent on some near horizon in the future.

Per the thesis of this book, that sustainability pursuits amplified during the pandemic, particularly through the push of digital innovation, it was indeed in the middle of the pandemic that Toyota launched its first climate fund in 2021. Adler shared,

> Toyota unearthed this idea that, we would like to do in climate technologies what Toyota Ventures has done in frontier technologies—basically, crowdsource the best thinking in startups, especially where Toyota is not looking now. Toyota is doing a ton of work in sustainability, electrification, and hydrogen—all these things. But the fund can find things where Toyota is not looking.

Large multinational companies must leverage open innovation. Crowdsourcing as much as possible through a venture fund allows the company access to the kind of innovations that are going to create breakthrough step changes in how we address such critical sustainability as climate change.

At the same time, the pandemic (and the digital innovation it catalyzed), enabled corporations to access startup talent to power the ventures that, pre-pandemic, used to be centered around the incumbent hubs. As Adler explained,

That's part of what has spun up these investment flywheels in Silicon Valley and in Israel. There's a sort of localization bias, and therefore the talent tends to only be plumbed from local areas. I always struggled with the idea that there are brilliant people elsewhere, but how do you get to them? The great thing about the pandemic was location didn't matter anymore. Everyone was on the same playing field—we were all interacting through Zoom.

Given Tracy Barba's background in impact investing in her previous role as Executive Director and Head of Responsible Investment for 500 Global, her take on the growth of corporate ventures into ESG comes with empirical wisdom. "I think we're still in the very early days for venture and ESG," she said,

so there's just a lot of unknowns that are still out there. But the theory of change is that if you can start early enough to integrate these values to help companies figure out how they start to do this from the very beginning, then you have a greater chance of success, so when they get to be larger and become the next Facebook and Google of the world, they will already be thinking about this.

Barba believes the shift is in motion, citing,

Canva is a good example. They're just doing a tremendous job all the way around in terms of their environmental commitments, and also their social diversity and employee ownership commitments. If we could see more of those kinds of unicorns, that would make it all worthwhile. But I think we're just in the early days.

In this context, investing in sustainability or ESG factors is not just about institutional investors investing in external funds or stocks that have the ESG rigor in place, but also about organizations making investments into their own operations for ESG hygiene, transparency, and hence overall risk management.

SHIFTING FUNDING PARADIGMS

Jason Salfi from Dimensional Energy has a first-hand view of how investment has changed in the past few years around the pandemic.

"There's a lot of early money coming towards early-stage companies of our size and stature," Salfi observed.

> The floodgates are open. Money is more accessible. There are more brand name funds that have a lot of money devoted to startups. Governments have turned their lens. Their attention is on companies like ours, funding companies like ours on up. It's a time unlike any other that we can get support.

Salfi noted he was able to raise US$3 million in series C capital in 2021, in addition to US$7 million in grant funding from the Department of Energy, because of where Dimensional Energy was in terms of development. The digital innovation around the proxy for face-to-face communications—Zoom, Teams, and the like—eased access to funding and helped him concentrate his efforts in energy.

> I was suddenly forced to consolidate my efforts to my basement, my office here, downstairs in our house. Previously, when I would fundraise, I would go to a conference. I would meet someone in New York, meet someone in San Francisco, meet someone in Houston—wherever—and look them in the eye, tell them why they should give me a million dollars. That takes so much time and energy to get on a plane. This time, I raised $3 million from my basement—and our investors were all over the world. We have partners from South Korea, a consortium from London and Greece. We have another group from Houston, a couple of folks on the West Coast, and in Oklahoma. People from all over the world invested in Dimensional Energy last year, and I didn't leave my basement.

The pandemic lowered the barriers toward ways of doing business—including the historically high touch nature of venture funding. Plus, the sense of all being in it together—all facing the same limitations, all working from home and remotely—helped level the playing field even beyond simply a greater availability of funding for startups like Dimensional Energy.

David Ellington, the founder of the Silicon Valley Blockchain Society (SVBS), witnessed the emergence of novel financing channels driven by digital innovations during the pandemic. Through his work in harnessing blockchain technology, Ellington combined community dynamics and digital innovation with transformation in investment products to create greater access to value creation. The mission of SVBS is succinctly expressed in three words: "Fund the revolution." They aim to invest in entrepreneurs building DeFI-related or Web3.0-related technologies, companies, or platforms—whether it is in artificial intelligence, Internet of Things (IoT), fintech, or even space-related ventures. Their focus is on frontier technologies, analyzing and supporting teams that have great ideas and the capability to execute them.

Ellington challenged the idea that digital innovations and communication transformation had democratized access to wealth within the traditional context. While there may be more sources of capital available for entrepreneurs to pitch their ideas, he believed that the big traditional players were not necessarily changing their investment decisions to democratize the process. Instead, he observed a global trend where more people around the world decided to create their own ecosystems, moving away from simply copying the Silicon Valley model.

In line with this, Larry Fink, in his 2020 letter, predicted that the next wave of unicorns—highly successful startups—would be "sustainable, scalable innovators – startups that help the world decarbonize and make the energy transition affordable for all consumers." This shift toward impactful and sustainable ventures reflects the changing landscape and priorities in the investment and entrepreneurial community.

ESG Funding Is the New ~~Black~~ Green

In 2005, Rachel Payne was part of the founding team of Google.org's First Hire—the first corporate hybrid philanthropic and investment fund, with a value of around US$1 billion. First Hire focused on climate change and global development. While in graduate school at Stanford Business School in the early 2000s, she was interested in studying social ventures and understanding sustainable models for economic empowerment and for sustainable development. Payne had a front seat on the ways large enterprises are shifting their focus and the kinds of investments they are now making. "It was in that vein that I later became interested in a CSR role and later joined Google.org. I bring that up because at the time— this was back in 2005, 2006—the term impact investing was just being invented" Payne recalled,

> It was still very early for the field, and we often saw that impact investors were viewed as purely philanthropic with concessionary returns. There

wasn't a lot of pressure for large asset allocators to invest either endowments from foundations or universities in line with their core program strategies. And there also wasn't really any pressure on Wall Street around ESG.

Payne noted,

> Over time, that's changed dramatically. There are several forcing functions for that. The biggest one, of course, that has been the slowest to move is climate change and the existential threat that presents. It wasn't really until COVID, when business as usual was completely upended when people were forced to reorganize everything from the way they do their work to the nature of their work itself, and they had to pull back—especially with the disruption of supply chains. It gave space and time for a rethinking of everything.

In Payne's mind, COVID-19 made it more painfully evident that there were, and are, vulnerabilities in the lifecycle of our global economy. And, with this magnification, came a greater correlation between ESG factors and risk, which then has a material impact on enterprise performance— which in turn gets regulators involved.

Payne commented,

> This zoomed in on some of these global risk factors that could further disrupt performance, that need to be called out more. As we've seen, the SEC has put forward a statement regarding climate disclosures being a requirement. That's a major move for institutionalizing climate reporting in a way that's consistent, but also gives potential investors and existing shareholders an opportunity to understand the full set of risk factors.

Mona ElNaggar, a prominent leader in the field, has been actively involved in the ESG space as co-founder and partner of Valo Ventures. Valo Ventures is a mission-driven venture capital firm that focuses on three catalyzing megatrends that are shaping our world today - climate change, circular economy, and empowered people. ElNaggar's impressive career began at Morgan Stanley, where she played a pivotal role in cofounding the technology investment banking practice in London. She also led non-US investing for TIFF Investment Management, a global asset management firm specializing in outsourced CIO talent and private equity investment solutions for foundations and charitable organizations. ElNaggar brings a unique perspective on the evolution of fundraising, both pre-pandemic and during the pandemic. With her extensive background and expertise, she can shed light on the significant changes that have occurred in funding dynamics and the impact of increased availability of capital within the ESG space.

When ElNaggar moved back to the United States, she began to hear a growing prevalence of ESG and social impact topics discussed among underlying investors.

> These investors were increasingly concerned about the dissonance between what they were doing with their grants and how their endowments were being invested. And they were expressing a growing misalignment between their desired social impact and how their endowments were invested, saying, "We're trying to support the environment with our grants, but you have our endowment invested in coal. So how do we square that circle?"

The generally accepted view in the endowment management world was that fiduciaries needed to focus only on maximizing profit, but ElNaggar and her partners at Valo saw another way.

> "We believed that combining purpose and profit was not only possible, but that we didn't have to choose between them. In fact, these two possibilities supported each other. You can't have a truly sustainable venture that lacks a profit motive, but also that vision, that sense of a greater social and environmental purpose was not only indispensable, but had directed some of the best organizations we'd ever been involved with," ElNaggar said..

Valo Ventures was founded to invest at the intersection between purpose and profit and the role we can play in cultivating a sustainable existence on this planet.

ElNaggar recalled that when Valo began, some would mistake the idea of impact investing with an acceptance of lower returns, which is far from the case.

Valo worked to dissipate this perception and instead demonstrate that profit combined with purpose are mutually reinforcing rather than mutually exclusive.

> If we can look back and see that we have had a tertiary impact by bringing see that we have brought other people others into this space as wellasparea

through making impactful investments with strong returns – that will be an even bigger win indeed to get more investors caring about the big challenges of our lifetime. by being good investors and showing that our investments with this ESG lens can lead to good returns, that will have been a good thing. There's so much that needs to be done andthat we need to continue attracting that more capital towards high-impact solutions come in."

While more investors and corporations have pivoted to impact investing in recent years, especially during the pandemic—many are still finding their footing while walking the line between impact and returns.

ElNaggar observed that some of these newcomers were increasingly from the traditional world of investment, firms not known for ESG tendencies. She gave a nod to her own husband, who also works in venture capital, as a prime example of the shift. One of her husband's partners reached out to ElNaggar saying, "Hey, we're looking at something around offsets." She gladly offered her support and knowledge, recognizing the positive impact of more capital flowing into ESG-focused investments. ElNaggar expressed enthusiasm about the growing involvement of smart enterprise software investors like her husband's firm coming into the space, highlighting the positive implications of increased capital infusion from an investor's perspective.

Jim Adler from Toyota Ventures also observed the shifting landscape of investments into new ventures happening in Silicon Valley and beyond. "It's huge," he insisted.

> There are now trillions of dollars sloshing around. In a sense, there's not enough quality startups to absorb the capital, which is unfortunate because I don't want to see so many failures that people lose face. But it's a high-class problem. This is not like Clean Tech 1.0 when there were plenty of ideas, but not enough capital, not enough pull-through, and not enough market demand. The hope is this time, with Clean Tech 2.0, there is enough market demand—enough belief to really scale these technologies, to capitalize them, and then scale them.

Sure enough, McKinsey calculated that in 2022, about US$270 billion had been raised in capital for ESG efforts—nearly triple the figure in the pre-pandemic year of 2019 (see Figure 5.2).[5] And the numbers continue to grow. The investment shifts that happened during the pandemic have not been to the scale we need (yet), but it is trending in the right direction.

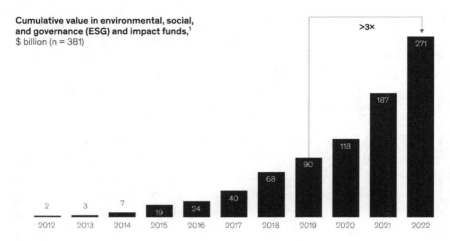

Cumulative value in environmental, social,
and governance (ESG) and impact funds,[1]
$ billion (n = 381)

>3x

¹Cumulative final closed size in ESG, climate, Sustainable Finance Disclosure Regulation, and impact buyout or infrafunds where fund size has been disclosed.
Source: PitchBook; McKinsey analysis

FIGURE 5.2
Cumulative value in ESG and impact funds

EVERYTHING, EVERYWHERE, ALL AT ONCE (?)

The pandemic had the effect of disrupting so much of everything, everywhere, all at once, that in the din of it all, as Rachel Payne put it in our interview, "you could actually reimagine that we could organize ourselves in new ways, we could channel capital in new ways."

The pandemic also had a way of foreshadowing what would be down the road in terms of a major global crisis. As Payne also added,

> If COVID-19 is any indication of what a crisis looks like on a global scale, climate change is going to be much worse. So, it became almost analogous to what the climate crisis is going to do—with the difference that the climate crisis has been a long time coming.

One major impact of all of this, with respect to the investment community, of course, is the continued shift away from fossil fuels.

> It really highlighted that continuing to invest in oil and gas is not a long-term winning strategy. There may still be some short-term gains, especially right now because of the way that OPEC is playing the markets. But if you think about the long-term reality, having to have SEC-required climate

disclosures and every company now expected to have a climate statement (as well as their overall ESG statement), is putting a new level of accountability and pressure at an institutional level that's never been done before.

As funding moves away from fossil fuel, the funds become available and can be directed toward other alternative investments, with funds that factor in for ESG gaining more mindshare.

This increase in available funding is opening truly exciting developments in sustainability. George Coelho, who started his remarkable career as an innovator and investor with Intel Ventures, brought up the death of soil in our conversation. Because so much of modern agriculture has been extractive and pulled more nutrients out of the soil than it put back, in many places, the land has been overused. "You stick in more fertilizers, such as nitrogen, but in many places, the soil is dead. You're not going to get more out of it. You're getting less out of it."

As a result, Coelho said, "You have to regenerate agriculture, which is restoring the balance of the Earth and the nutrients of the Earth." He puts the onus for such changes on investors: "Financial investors like us have to help the planet recover by measuring things and making sure that the investments you make help the Earth and are truly impactful." This isn't quite the same as ESG, broadly speaking, Coehlo says, although that's the umbrella, but rather, "It's impactful, which means we have to have financial and impact returns for each of our deals."

These kinds of investments have the sort of real-world application the pandemic helped show us is so important, Coehlo noted.

> Now we're saving people's lives. Are you eating healthier food? Is that food right for you? Can you figure out a malaria outbreak? Can you figure out a COVID outbreak? Can you test people for COVID, and other diseases quickly in remote areas? Yes, you can.

The pandemic, and the sense of urgency around sustainability it helped magnify, leveled up the challenge for investors and venture-founders alike. The challenge is to solve exceedingly complex and seemingly insurmountable threats. Added Coehlo, "That's revolutionary. That is how you measure impact."

The increasing focus on ESG and sustainability-related value, along with the substantial funds being allocated to support such initiatives, has brought transparency to the forefront. Investors now demand data-driven insights to make informed decisions. Payne highlighted the Institutional Investors Group on Climate Change, which represents a staggering US$48 trillion in assets under management, and their commitment to require comprehensive climate disclosures. They played a pivotal role in advocating for new SEC requirements and establishing frameworks and toolkits to aid companies in transitioning to a net-zero future. In our conversation she insisted, "that's the big change that I saw—that it became real, it became serious, it became required. There was accountability, and there's a demand for more transparency." This heightened accountability and demand for transparency have led to a significant shift in the way sustainability is perceived and pursued.

Christine Tiballi echoed these sentiments, noting that the pandemic brought long-standing climate issues and opportunities to the forefront. She emphasized,

> I do think that the level of investment in climate tech has jumped significantly. COVID helped to push that to the forefront of people's minds and discussions. I also think that there was an important parallel shift, which was the financial potential of climate starting to be borne out. There were sort of two things happening at the same time.

These parallel shifts have further propelled the importance of sustainability and climate-conscious investing in today's landscape.

Sound Infrastructure for Sound Investing

According to Caroline Chan, Vice President of Intel's Network and Edge Solution Group and General Manager of the Network Business Integration Division, the key to success in achieving diversified funding and talent lies in investing in fundamental infrastructure. Throughout her career, which spans developments in network solutions, IoT expansion into new verticals, promoting equity for women in technology, and bridging the digital divide, Chan has observed the transformative power of such investments. Chan noted that supply chain issues during the pandemic helped highlight the need for this infrastructure. She used refrigerator trucks driving cross-country as an example.

> Now they're able to tell when the trucks actually leave the port of LA to drive to the East Coast. That's kind of the planning information people

need, and they didn't have the data. The supply chain constraints of the pandemic also triggered this kind of action.

A significant challenge around infrastructure needs manifested when children were forced into remote education, and some lacked access to the necessary resources. In response to a request for help from a housing project in Sacramento, Chan and her team sought funding from the Intel Foundation. Thanks to the grant funding received, they were able to build a private Citizens Broadband Radio Service (CBRS) network in the area where most of the children lived.

Not only did it transform the lives of the students, but it also positively influenced their entire families. Afterward, there was a video testimonial about the project that clearly illuminated how the endeavor "did not just transform these kids' lives, but their entire families," proclaimed Chan. The success of this initiative highlights the importance of investing in fundamental infrastructure to empower communities and create opportunities for diversified funding and talent to thrive.

Chan continued with another first-hand narrative involving farmers in North Dakota who were struggling with the impacts of climate change. By leveraging 5G sensors, the farmers were able to fine-tune their agricultural water needs, leading to improved yields and agricultural efficiency. Microsoft's ongoing testing of seed types and refining of agricultural science further supported this endeavor.

Chan emphasized the importance of data in agriculture, stating that providing data back to the growers and seed companies was immensely helpful in improving yields. This not only positively impacted the livelihood of the farmers but also contributed to food security for the entire country. As she said,

> If you have the data, if you can analyze the data and provide data back to the growers, back to the seed companies—it's a tremendous help to improve the yield. That means life for the farmers and food security for our country.

Additionally, Intel was involved in funding a private network for the Utah Inland Port Authority (IPA), which plays a crucial role in coordinating communication between airports, railroads, and other transportation hubs in Utah. The IPA is vital for the state's economy, as up to 40% of Utah's GDP runs through it, and a substantial portion of employment and incomes is dependent on the logistics system.

The private network, covering 16,000 acres, was aimed at providing asset tracking capabilities, ensuring security, and promoting sustainability in the region. Through strategic partnerships with the state and other technology partners, Intel aimed to bring enhanced connectivity and efficient asset management to support Utah's economic and logistical growth.

Digital infrastructure investment pays key dividends, especially with the role that digital innovation has played in helping communities and businesses manage risk and achieve sustainability outcomes. Chan pointed to portable telecom infrastructure—such as what was used in Puerto Rico after Hurricane Maria in 2017, when NTT and Verizon airlifted in suitcase networks—"a suitcase that contained an entire private 5G network, with the ability to do satellite uplink and downlink." As Chan recalled, "The emergency workers had no idea how bad the damages were outside of the capital; they had no way of even traveling there. But this is a suitcase that can be airdropped and can actually bring itself up online an hour." Investment in those kinds of technologies can be life-changing—and, in Puerto Rico, it was.

BACK TO BASICS

When people hear "infrastructure," especially with respect to digital innovation, they may tend to think of technology platform. In our interviews, we also addressed the less glossy side of infrastructure— essential living infrastructure, from housing to mobility. Xavone Charles, a Managing Partner at Desert Elite Management, brought his background in architecture and development to our conversation. As we have been uncovering, the pandemic shed light on a socioeconomic divide of which many were already aware—especially in the affordable housing space— but that didn't always translate to the right kind of action. To Charles's mind, a lot of the investment that was theoretically made in response to that heightened societal understanding of the socioeconomic divide was, in actuality, throwing money to placate stakeholders rather than driving strategic development and actual systemic change.

Charles used the example of electric vehicles—which, he noted, are irrelevant if your basic needs are not being met. That is, to his mind, the biggest issue with infrastructure investment. If it is not made with people's basic needs in mind, it will likely continue to leave people behind. He explained, "The next ten years are about preservation for humanity," because, without drastic change, the challenges around climate impact, socio-political unrest, social injustice, and inequities, may eventually become insurmountable.

INVESTING IN GEOPOLITICAL INFRASTRUCTURE

We have covered several key issues related to the importance of private–public initiatives toward sustainability. Here we zoom in on the geopolitics hanging in the balance across different segments of the world. When looking at risk, the Russian invasion of Ukraine highlights key aspects of risk that were likely not so obvious before 2022. In this especially horrifying scenario, the sustainability of a country's own sovereignty within a region (seemingly suddenly) tied aspects of regional economic vulnerabilities, food supply, energy scarcity, cybersecurity, and other critically interconnected aspects of societal integrity into another Petri dish of global fragility. Fortunately, the digitalization journey that Ukraine had already undertaken, and which was accelerated by the pandemic, is enabling the country to effectively defend its sovereignty, while catalyzing investments into the ingredients of this Petri dish—with all roads leading to sustainability of not just a country, but the hyperconnected globe.

In our interview with Diana Rakus, head of Ukraine's Ministry of Digital Transformation, we explored this intersection of sustainability, digital transformation, and investment (in this case as a national imperative). COVID-19 absolutely catalyzed profound digital transformation for Ukrainian people and communities—like how digitalization helped communities and businesses survive the pandemic everywhere. Yet, the connectivity and digital access driven by the ministry ended up inadvertently having a profound impact on how Ukrainians were equipped and empowered to respond to the Russian invasion.

Rakus noted the pandemic meant a greater focus on digital solutions, because of how everyone was stuck at home, including transitioning to online processes, applications, etc., and more. Because of Ukraine's investment in digital infrastructure, anyone can watch the news through an app. That investment has played a crucial role in fighting the Russian invasion. Not only has it aided intelligence gathering (such as Russian troop reporting), but Ukrainians' increased digital and media literacy allow them to fight misinformation and use their phones as a tool of resistance. Rakus noted they have even made it possible for Ukrainians to leverage simple game mechanisms on their phones to thwart Russian web and cyber operations. That speaks to an important point—the way in which the will of the people and innovation in communications can be more powerful than a mass of weapons. The long-term goal of the Ministry of Digital Transformation, Rakus said, is to make Ukraine the IT hub of Eastern Europe. That requires help from the outside world, too, and more of the world coming together.

Investing in the digital innovation in the case of Ukraine has been an essential part of defense and sovereign sustainability. But it should not just be dedicated to a nationalist agenda. Rakus said,

> We absolutely unite and share the same principles and share the same values. We really would like to have more help. We need more protection, more support, real support—not only words and long discussions. The situation showed us again that we have very little time to make any decisions. We should be proactive in order to develop and in order to guarantee all the things that we promised for our citizen—for citizens of the whole world. Because it's hard to believe and hard to understand this invasion.

Rakus encouraged,

> Even right now, sometimes it looks like just a horror dream. It's hard to believe and hard to explain that it's the 21st century. Having all these technologies and having all these international treaties and duties of countries here with the obligation to avoid wars … we should be focusing on how we protect each other and create conditions for global sustainability—not as separate independent counties, but as a whole planet and a shared ecosystem.

Checking the Boxes, or Meaningful and Authentic?

During the pandemic, as ESG and sustainability gained greater prominence, there was a significant frustration over the approach taken by many. It seemed that actions, including investments from external stakeholders and within organizations, were often superficial, merely checking a box without embracing a genuine and authentic shift in mindset.

Rene Haas, CEO of ARM, expressed a healthy dose of caution regarding the motions made in the investment and analyst community. He admitted,

> I don't know if they truly care at the end of the day. Dealing with Wall Street or London financiers, they want to ask the right questions, ensure your company represents the right values, and check those boxes. But not at the expense of operating income, EBITDA, or operating margin growth—those are the boxes they truly prioritize.

Haas acknowledged a shift in direction but emphasized the need for further diligence.

> We still have a way to go until investors truly emphasize sustainability as a key differentiator between companies on the margin. If two companies have similar financial metrics but one has a significantly higher commitment to sustainability, then, yes, investors might care on the margin. However, the cynical part of me says that they still prioritize financials above all else.

Nevertheless, Haas did confide that ARM is continuing to focus on R&D for the chip industry that will make investments more meaningful and impactful in both the near- and longer-term horizon, such that as the silicon chip industry continues to grow with the surge of digitalization catalyzed by the pandemic, ARM will be a steward for how technological breakthroughs will advance the sustainability agenda.

Mona ElNaggar from Valor Ventures noted,

> I think it is great that Larry Fink [of BlackRock] said ESG risk is investment risk. Many of the big money managers—the venture funds, the private equity funds—they're following what their investors are saying. When you see these funds develop these new climate sub-funds or ESG sub-funds, they're not always doing it because they really believe in it.

And that is okay. It is okay that they are being pushed that way by shareholders, partners, customers, and employees—so long as it pushes the agenda in a way that momentum becomes irreversible.

Meanwhile, the momentum bodes well for innovative startups. ElNaggar noted, 90% of global GDP is committed to net zero and governments are increasingly regulating higher standards, so it is now on all of us to develop the tools to make that real. "If these groups are to stop using single-use packaging or demand a higher proportion of recycled content in batteries, start-up ecosystem has to develop and deploy new solutions and the venture community needs to finance them."

Investing in All Resources—Including Human

During the initial phase of the pandemic, Rahul Sekhon served as the Chief Technology Officer at Sun Life, a financial services company committed to promoting financial security and better health for individuals. Sekhon observed that ESG investment is part of a broader cultural shift aimed at advancing social sustainability, particularly in relation to the health and well-being of employees.

He shared an interesting conversation with the CEO of a cooperative who was planning to increase their ESG investing from 20% to 60%, with a long-term goal of reaching 100%. In addressing the necessary cultural change within the organization, Sekhon emphasized the importance of utilizing their talented workforce effectively. He prompted them with,

> When we were discussing this aspect of what they need to do to bring in the needed cultural change within their organization to address the change that's in front of them, that's the first thing which we focused on, which is you've got great talent. Are you using them effectively? Are you giving them enough capacity to stop doing certain things so they can start learning new things? Or are you thinking that what you've got is not good enough?

Sekhon's insight aligns with other discussions that emphasized the significance of organizations effectively supporting and engaging their human capital effectively during the pandemic. Those organizations that recognize the value of their employees and foster a culture of mutual understanding will be better equipped to thrive in the future.

That can and should be the reality for organizations investing in human capital. Invest in your people to ensure that not only is their work culture sustainable, but also that they believe that the organization is investing in them, and that their capabilities are limitless.

Will the Money-Music Come to an End, Post-Pandemic?

During the pandemic, the correlation between risk, financial sustainability, and ESG factors became more evident, leading to increased investments in funds that integrated these considerations. However, we are also witnessing the politicization of ESG and a subsequent backlash, particularly in the United States. An example of this is when Republican Governor Ron DeSantis of Florida successfully proposed banning "social, political, or ideological interests" in investment decisions for the state's pension funds in August 2022.

Given these developments, questions arise regarding the sustainability of the momentum toward ESG investments. How long will this trend last? Will it endure the challenges posed by political debates and changing regulatory landscapes?

Jim Adler from Toyota added a relevant note of rational caution in our conversation with him, "We're seeing the capital arrive. The capital is here, but if the returns aren't there, the capital could dry up." He went on to note how ESG investment (in the form of cleaner energy) might also offer an opportunity to reduce petrochemical dependence. "It could be incredibly important for global stability for energy to be generated locally, if at all possible. There's a petrochemical dependence that is destabilizing, not just for our planet, but for our politics too."

ElNagger similarly acknowledged, "Investors can make these commitments," she said, "but they need to find ways to meet those commitments. And so the money follows demand, whether it's corporate demands of things that they need to buy, or investor demand of how they want their money deployed."

Financial markets are no stranger to trends, particularly in the realm of innovation and technology. The key question is whether the surge in interest toward ESG investments is driven by a genuine analysis of the correlation between sustainability and financial performance, or if it's primarily influenced by the fear of missing out (FOMO) or following popular movements.

According to ElNaggar, there is currently a significant influx of capital available in the market. While occasional imbalances may arise, the market tends to find its equilibrium as supply meets demand. However, she believes that this situation may not persist indefinitely. "While the market person in me thinks there are occasional periods of imbalance, supply eventually meets demands. Even if that's a temporary thing," she said. As a result, investors who are proactive in embracing ESG funding might discover that they are ahead of the curve, particularly when compared to those who continue to rely solely on traditional profit measures.

MAKING SURE WE LEARN FROM THIS

Could we extract valuable insights from the increased prominence of ESG in the investment landscape during the pandemic? When we spoke with Tracy Barba, she observed, "One of the things I hear a lot in discussions now with ESG is how should we have prepared for that? How would the ESG lens have prepared us better? Could it have prepared us for unexpected sorts of things like that?" Given the changing face, literally, of the world accelerated impacts to organic and inorganic ecosystems, such occurrences are no longer entirely unforeseen.

Barba insisted,

> We need to be thinking more about these risks as actuals, not only the financial risks associated with them. They're not a probability: there's a likelihood that they will happen. How are we going to then deal with them? Then how do we account for that—both on the risk side and the opportunity side—as we're investing in companies that are developing solutions?

The pandemic has accentuated the need to understand how new ventures are addressing these risks that are not necessarily novel in occasion, but rather in our understanding of them.

Barba believes it will take time before we can establish the necessary metrics, indices, and standards for better due diligence. She indicated. "I think those are things that we're still grappling with, and more data will tell over time. We're relatively still new in the ESG space." While there have been opportunities for companies to greenwash, she said, "It's complicated and a little messy, and we're still building. It's going to take some time before we figure out what it is we need to measure and how we place value. But I think we're getting closer to it."

The drive toward smarter investments is evident across all sectors and industries. For instance, Kevin Grayling, an executive at Florida Crystals, emphasizes their commitment to becoming a leader in their industry while actively seeking carbon and greenhouse gas reductions. Grayling explained,

> We have an ambition to be a leader in our industry—and not just in our industry, but in manufacturing deals with carbon reductions or green-house gas reductions. So, we are investing hundreds of millions of dollars over the next few years to experiment with renewable sources of energy in the processing of sugar, to deal with any waste that comes out of processing that raw sugar into refined sugars, and all the way through to our brands and our packaging.

By investing in renewable energy sources and sustainable practices throughout their operations, including packaging and waste management, organizations are positioning themselves to remain relevant, and to future-proof their organization.

Meanwhile, unintended unsustainable consequences of the pandemic, like more waste, brought the need for innovation toward sustainability into sharper view. Grayling pointed to the mountain of garbage and plastics generated during the pandemic, e.g., masks, takeout containers, plastic gloves, test kit materials, and more. "It's probably hard to imagine just how much additional plastic was created as part of the pandemic," he reflected. "Necessity is a great source of invention. I think what you'll see is an acceleration of investment into areas that can make these things more sustainable in general, and for the next time that this happens." Executives like Grayling are focusing on various facets of sustainability to safeguard their organizations' future and adapt to the ever-evolving landscape of their industry and human civilization as a whole.

> *When the last tree has been cut down, the last fish caught, the last river poisoned, only then will we realize that one cannot eat money.*
>
> **– American Indian Proverb**

As the initial panic and chaos caused by COVID-19 begins to subside, we are witnessing a mixed response in the market regarding ESG and sustainability investing. The term "ESG" has been somewhat tarnished in the traditional investment landscape due to its politicization in the United States. However, at the state and government levels in major regions, particularly in the European Union, there has been a significant push toward investing in ESG initiatives. This has led to the growth of private–public partnerships dedicated to sustainable outcomes.

The hope and expectation are that the paradigm shift triggered during the pandemic will yield significant results in the coming decade—results that go beyond financial metrics such as balance sheets, multipliers, and exits. The focus will also be on other value measurements that take into account the impact on the Earth, human health, safety, and more. This holistic approach to investment holds the promise of creating long-lasting positive change in various aspects of our world.

NOTES

1. UBS. (n.d). *How Has COVID-19 Impacted ESG Investing?* Retrieved January 2, 2023, from https://www.ubs.com/uk/en/assetmanagement/insights/investment-outlook/panorama/panorama-mid-year-2020/articles/covid-19-impacted-esg-investing.html)
2. Oikonomoum I., & Zhou, X. (2016, January). ESG shareholder engagement and downside risk. *SSRN Electronic Journal.* https://www.researchgate.net/profile/Xiaoyan-Zhou-7/publication/318002428_ESG_Shareholder_Engagement_and_Downside_Risk/links/5e6769ce299bf1744f6f12f6/ESG-Shareholder-Engagement-and-Downside-Risk.pdf
3. McKinsey & Co. (2017, October 25). *From 'Why' to 'Why Not': Sustainable Investing as the New Normal.* https://www.mckinsey.com/industries/private-equity-and-principal-investors/our-insights/from-why-to-why-not-sustainable-investing-as-the-new-normal
4. Fink, L. (2022). *Larry Fink's 2022 Letter to CEOs: The Power of Capitalism.* BlackRock. https://www.blackrock.com/corporate/investor-relations/larry-fink-ceo-letter
5. McKinsey & Co. (2023, March 13). *Climate Investing: Continuing Breakout Growth Through Uncertain Times.* https://www.mckinsey.com/capabilities/sustainability/our-insights/climate-investing-continuing-breakout-growth-through-uncertain-times

6

In Closing for Me, but an Opening for You

AS THE NIGHTMARE BECOMES AN EVER-DISTANT MEMORY

While the pandemic brought the world to a momentary standstill and launched an existential threat to our physical and mental health and livelihood, it also catalyzed a focus and mainstreaming of Environmental, Social, and Governance (ESG) and sustainability—much of it fueled by digital innovations that powered the ways to survive and thrive through an unprecedented upheaval of humankind.

I am eternally thankful to have found like-minds among diverse community, corporate venture, academic, and government leaders whom we interviewed to explore the merits of the thesis that the pandemic, together with digital innovations, amplified the sustainability imperative all around the world. I am grateful to have had a window into multiple vectors of society, and to experience a gamut of expressions in our conversations. Delight, sadness, frustration, surprise, anger, laughter, disbelief, passion, despair, and peace—you name it, it was peppered in our Zoom and Teams sessions. It all culminated in a new perspective of purpose, along with a sense that we are on the brink of a new era, perhaps even an epoch.

We can look beyond the "Black Swan" of the pandemic and be inspired by the possibilities that the challenges—to communities, governments, industries and enterprises, and investments—have unlocked. A broader

DOI: 10.4324/9781003462347-6

sense of the interconnectedness of people and the natural world around us, greater mental health awareness, enhanced understanding of social safety nets, deeper understanding of community health, supply chains, and so much more—these are all "White Swan" moments of the pandemic.

WHERE INNOVATIVE TECHNOLOGY RUBBER HITS THE SUSTAINABILITY ROAD

At the heart of the pandemic was accelerated digitalization, and the sidecar of innovation, initially for sheer survivability, and now a perpetuating machine toward Smart "X" (Smart Cars, Smart Homes, Smart Cities, etc., etc.). With rapidly expanded connectivity and the commensurate explosion of data, blockchain decentralization, and a heavy dollop of machine learning algorithms, we have catapulted ourselves into a paradox of an energy-hungry technology environment that also may constitute the very salve that will save us from ourselves.

Meanwhile, as much as we possibly can, we do have to share and distribute innovation equitably. The great digitalization of the pandemic has lessened the degrees of separation among us, and that in turn means that for any one of us to benefit from innovations that have accelerated in the past few years, everyone must have access and reap the benefits, too. As long as we can be intentional in our communities and the decisions we make as individuals, as business leaders, and as community leaders, the dynamics multiply exponentially and can create unimaginable impact.

WHAT MIGHT THIS LOOK LIKE FOR LEADERS?

How does embracing ESG and "White Swan" moments change corporate culture, decision-making matrices, and the fundamentals of next-generation leadership—in communities and industry? How does it change the company values those business leaders choose to prioritize? In what ways might the most senior corporate leaders and their boards recalibrate vision and mission, in a way that considers this next era of stakeholder capitalism? The pandemic has helped us realize the ways that our professional lives need to fulfill us and help us feel that we are a part of an inclusive community even within an enterprise and that our employers are contributing to a brighter future. Through the effects of the pandemic, business leaders have a better-informed way of responding to the communities within the organization, and within the ecosystem in which they operate. They can better respond to this enhanced yearning for purpose and impact, and the way that we might redefine the value of work and "growth."

FOR LOCAL AND GLOBAL ECONOMIES TO PONDER

Funds are available at an unprecedented scale for sectors in economies that are investing in sustainability. This will reshape current and future corporate strategy and roadmaps for organizations. We see energy companies more energetically embracing renewable practices—both because they are becoming more affordable, and because that is what stakeholders and consumers seek as a way for the collective economy to realize more value beyond monetary profit.

This brings me to a thought-provoking proposition that has been brewing in my mind since the start of my research for this book, and encountering some of the writings of Albert Bartlett, a PhD in Physics who taught at universities in the United States and argued in class in papers that "sustainable growth" is an oxymoron.[1] It is one that I am contemplating presenting formally to the UN and pertains to the need for a redesign of the UN SDG number eight, called "Decent Work and Economic Growth" (Figure 6.1).[2] First, what does "Decent Work" even mean considering the economic diversity of global communities, as well within the context of a post-pandemic decade? Moreover, might we need to rethink the pursuit of "Economic Growth" that does not pit profit against global "thrive-ability." Goal #8, I muse these days that the words to use might be "Regenerative Growth", that would capture the goodness out of circular economy pursuits while also encouraging net-positive value generation, versus simply recycling. Another replacement could be "Spiritual Growth" that could promote a mindset shift that supports valuations beyond those measures that are purely monetary. Once I have a reasonable and compelling alternative articulation for this goal, I can thank the Pandemic for the formal proposal to submit to the United Nations.

FIGURE 6.1
United Nations Sustainable Development Goal # 8

AGENCY AND ACCOUNTABILITY

Imagine a Web 3.0 community beyond the Black Swan era that belongs to both no one and everyone at the same time. A community where "White Swan sightings" are shared as a way to demonstrate both small and large-scale efforts to affect climate change, social inequities, poor governance, and more. My hope is that this community not only provides inspiration to others pursuing sustainability in their own lives, both personally and professionally, but also encourages companies and communities to reward that *intentionality* as much as the outcomes.

Toward the end of this research, the European Union (EU) announced the notion of a Carbon Tax—calculating a tax on goods and services being imported into the EU, based on the carbon footprint of said good or service. Conversely and in response, I would like to imagine a time, not too far from now, where (again, thanks to digitalization, technology, and AI) individuals and organizations gain favorable credit scores or ratings based on their contribution to White Swan moments, or in observation of "White Swan sightings."

Consider, for example, an eFico score (enhanced credit score) for consumers and eCredit Ratings from agencies levied to organizations, and maybe even nation states. Imagine that these ratings are managed through a decentralized community to maintain the authenticity and integrity of the algorithms that define the score (read: improved ratings cannot be bought or manipulated). Maybe this Web 3.0 community is a future project, influenced by feedback from you in the coming, days, weeks, and months. And whether we have the luxury of "years" to add to the end of the sentence will be entirely up to you, me, all of us.

WHERE DOES THIS LEAVE/WELCOME US AS INDIVIDUALS—YOU, ME, US?

As we conclude this specific journey, know that this end is just the beginning of how every individual impacts the greater whole. Consider what actioning "White Swans" of mainstream sustainability moments might look like for you and in your life at home, in business, in your community, and as part of your national culture. What choices are you already making, and what choices can you still make, before choices are made for you? Coming out of the pandemic, and realizing even more acutely the fragility of our lives, and of the greater world around us, the accountability of the sustainability imperative is more urgent that ever. As Barbara Adachi confided,

> I actually think the "White Swan" was opening up the dialogue that probably was never really public before. It was very private, or it would be between two people sitting in a room, but it wouldn't become a board agenda item. It wouldn't become a topic of importance to the whole company,

and as we see to every member of diverse communities and economies.

So here we go—opening the windows and doors to the room, and putting a microphone not between these "two people" but for other individuals like you to join in the conversation. Many people individually chose to reimagine, and in some cases, redesign their purpose and prioritize the things that were important to them as a result of how the pandemic affected them, their business, and their communities. As we continue to do that, we can, hopefully, correct course in short order to get to the next planetary era.

THE ORGANICALLY INTELLIGENT GENIE

I hope you found some resonance with the perspectives illuminated in these pages and recognized common experience. While the Black Swan ripples of COVID-19 fade into the past, we are hopeful that the surge toward sustainability mindsets and actions will remain—not because some of us are eternal optimists, but because they must. And I do believe that this will be fueled significantly by breakthrough digital innovation (especially AI) that better harnesses intelligence in all living organisms so that we create a new sustainable paradigm of existence. I dubbed these capabilities, and imperative, "Organic Intelligence™."

Just as I was finishing this manuscript (summer 2023), an article in the *Financial Times* caught my eye. Called, "Scientists believe they are on the brink of proving the Earth has entered a new era for the first time in 11,700 years," the article explains,

> Scientists believe they are on the brink of proving the Earth has entered a new era for the first time in 11,700 years with the advent of the Anthropocene epoch, or the point when humanity's influence on the planet's geologic become irreversible.

Basically, a lake in Toronto was confirmed as yielding the ultimate signs of what archeologists are calling the "Anthropocene." The discovery was of human-made markers like artificial radionuclides, combustion particles, neobiota (organisms in areas where they are not native), and organic pollutants—pointing to planetary change caused by "we, the people." Now, I have been speaking publicly about the Anthropocene for some time, within the context of using innovation to address sustainability ambitions, and I was enthralled to witness the mainstreaming of this concept as I was concluding my book research. While the article could be taken as yet another "doom and gloom" expression from popular media, it served to reinforce my belief that we are well on our way to another era of positive sustainability impacts thanks to technology and innovation. One where digital Artificial Intelligence supports critical breakthroughs in what I have deemed "Organic Intelligence"™ (OI). Marc Andreessen of the vaunted VC Andreessen Horowitz coined the phrase, "Software is eating the world."[3] As I continue to delve into this concept of OI, I am thinking that a follow-up to Andreesen might be "and Organic Intelligence can recreate the world."

The "genie" of digital transformation and innovation is out of the bottle. Now we just need to put it to work with our collective will, energy and conviction that tomorrow at least can be a more resilient one, and at best, one where all organic matter lives toward a balanced and equitable existence. This will be a topic we will explore and refine in a future compilation of insights. That next journey I expect will lead to designing a possible blueprint for the next era or epoch, as we must transform ourselves out of the Anthropocene as soon as, well not "humanly" but rather "organically," as possible and bring down to a new era. The global pandemic catalyzed a springboard towards a broader sustainable mindset, and digital innovations are fueling the momentum. We now have unprecedented possibilities beyond the Black Swan of COVID-19 to harmonize human existence with planetary prosperity. I hope you agree.

NOTES

1. https://www.resilience.org/stories/2009-11-06/dr-albert-bartletts-laws-sustainability/
2. https://www.un.org/sustainabledevelopment/news/communications-material/
3. https://a16z.com/2011/08/20/why-software-is-eating-the-world/

Index